The Parent's Guide to

Turning Your Teen Into

a Millionaire

Also by Christopher Carosa...

From Cradle to Retirement: The Child IRA

– How to Start a Newborn Baby on the Road to Comfortable Retirement While Still in a Cozy Cradle

Hey! What's My Number?

– How to Improve the Odds You Will Retire in Comfort

A Pizza The Action

– Everything I Ever Learned About Business I Learned by Working in a Pizza Stand at the Erie County Fair

401(k) Fiduciary Solutions

– Expert Guidance for 401(k) Plan Sponsors on How to Effectively and Safely Manage Plan Compliance and Investments by Sharing the Fiduciary Burden with Experienced Professionals

Due Diligence

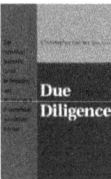

– The Individual Trustee's Guide to Selecting and Monitoring a Professional Money Manager

The Parent's Guide to Turning Your Teen Into a Millionaire

...and How to Do It Before

High School Graduation!

★ ★ ★ ★ ★

by

Christopher Carosa

Pandamensional Solutions, Inc.

Mendon, New York

Published by Pandamensional Solutions, Inc., Mendon, NY

Cover design by Catarina Lena Carosa

ISBN-10: 1-938465-10-5
ISBN-13: 978-1-938465-10-9

The Parent's Guide to Turning Your Teen Into a Millionaire

"Christopher Carosa has written several wonderful books that are terrific guides to securing our financial futures With his latest book, *The Parent's Guide to Turning Your Teen Into a Millionaire*, he has now given parents an outstanding gift to empower their children to have stable and enriched lives through the power of saving early and often with a mission to give them the financial ability to further their education without starting their adult lives living under the overwhelming burden of student loan debt. Chris has unlocked the key to growing wealth through compound interest in the most compelling and accessible way. He writes in such an engaging and informative way that it will be easy to put the path he lays out for his readers into immediate action. Investing your money is like planting a garden – the seeds need to be fed regularly so they will grow and grow and grow."

> Jamie Hammond, Producer, BizKid$, Seattle, Washington

"Look, the problem of squirrelling away enough for the winter season of our lives has been with us since life expectancies have exceeded our ability/desire to work, and while there is no shortage of articles about the looming retirement crisis, there are too few that offer constructive, actionable solutions. Chris has done a terrific job of thinking through and detailing a step-by-step, practical solution for you and me to put our next generation on the path to a financially secure retirement. His plan, like Archimedes dreamed of 'long enough lever,' takes ample advantage of compounding to do the heavy lifting of preparing for a successful life in retirement. His ideas will not only help you and your family, they will also help America.

> Drake Mosier, the inventor of 'robo-advice' and recipient of multiple awards in the retirement industry

From *FiduciaryNews.com* Articles:

"Here's an eye-opener sure to impress your teen or even pre-teen: Explain that every dollar they save today is worth $32 by the time they retire. The reason is compounding, most easily explained using the Rule of 72. It works like this: If you know what rate your money will earn in a year, just divide that number into 72. The result is how long it takes your savings to double. So, at 7.2%, an investment of $100 turns into $200 in 10 years. Over the following decade, that same $200 effortlessly becomes $400. Then it doubles again to $800 — with no extra weeds pulled and no more dogs walked. Eventually, it telescopes out to 32 times the money! The biggest advantage young investors have is time. Compounding is a powerful — and profitable — formula they can learn early on and use throughout their lives." (July 26, 2018)

> Scott Puritz, Managing Director at Rebalance in Bethesda, Maryland

"The younger you are when you start saving, the more you benefit from the power of compounding. If you have the means to contribute to any kind of savings account for a young child or grandchild, putting away even a small amount for that youngster now can pay off in spades by the time the child is of retirement age." (June 19, 2018)

> Rachel Sheedy, editor of Kiplinger's Retirement Report

"As long as a child (under the age of 18) has earned income they can contribute to a Child IRA. Whether it is weekend time spent at the family business, counseling at camp, or a paid summer internship, a child has the right to contribute to an IRA to offset any earned income." (March 5, 2019)

> Ben Soccodato, Financial Services Executive and Investment Advisor Representative at The SKG Team at Barnum Financial Group in Elmsford, New York

For middle-schoolers everywhere:
Listen to your parents after you convince them.

TABLE OF CONTENTS

Section One: The Dream

Section Two: The Child IRA – The Basic Idea Explained

Section Three: The Hows and Whys – Setting Up a Child IRA for Your Children and Grandchildren

Section Four: Your Step-by-Step Guide – Turn Your Teen Into a Millionaire Before High School Graduation!

Section Five: Bonus Chapters

Section Six: Appendices

FOREWORD

Christopher Carosa has written several wonderful books that are terrific guides to securing our financial futures. With his latest book, *The Parent's Guide to Turning Your Teen Into a Millionaire*, he has now given parents an outstanding gift to empower their children to have stable and enriched lives through the power of saving early and often with a mission to give them the financial ability to further their education without starting their adult lives living under the overwhelming burden of student loan debt. I am honored to write this short Forward to this amazing tool.

Chris has unlocked the key to growing wealth through Compound Interest in the most compelling and accessible way. He writes in such an engaging and informative way that it will be easy to put the path he lays out for his readers into immediate action. Investing your money is like planting a garden – the seeds need to be fed regularly so they will grow and grow and grow.

My partners and I have been delighted to produce our award-winning television series, "BizKid$", for the last 12 years to open kids eyes to how important it is to take charge of their financial futures as early as possible. Our mission was to engage kids though "edutainment" combining solid education with sketch comedy, animation, and profiles of young people from all over the country that have started their own for-profit or non-profit ventures from lemonade stands to creating a product that earned them more than a million dollars before they graduated from high school. We have shown how important it is to set financial goals; to start earning, saving and investing their money as early as they can.

In our TV episodes, we have demonstrated why it's a far better thing to save than to spend. We cover all the ins and outs of simple money management – setting short-term, medium-term and long-term goals, building a budget and sticking to it; making smart money decisions, such as PYF (pay yourself first) and using financial tools, like savings accounts and CD's that build their money through the power of compound interest.

Helping your kids understand the difference between Wants and Needs at an early age will be a great foundation for them in establishing healthy financial lives. Giving them the gift of learning good habits in dealing with the money they receive for birthdays, graduations, or even what they make from mowing the lawn or selling lemonade is so important to their future well-being.

I encourage you to read Chris' plan carefully and apply his guidance immediately. Following his plan of action will enable you to give your children an excellent lift off into their adult lives. It's also never too late to initiate Chris' ideas into your own plan to enrich your financial lives and give yourselves wonderful years enriched with multiple options when you are ready to retire. It's never too late to use the power of compound interest! Now get going!!

Jamie Hammond
Producer, BizKid$
Seattle, Washington

ACKNOWLEDGEMENTS

I was gratefully surprised by the response from readers when *From Cradle to Retirement: The Child IRA – How to start a newborn on the road to comfortable retirement while still in a cozy cradle* was first published in 2018. So were my publicists at Annie Jennings. Both Sara and Stacy quickly found interest and I was soon appearing on the airwaves from CNBC to FoxNews to Inc. Magazine to dozens of top-50 radio markets across the country.

You can image how happy it made me to share this easy concept. With a little bit of work (literally!), every infant can become a millionaire. There's no need to change existing laws. There's no need to come up with a one-in-a-million idea. There's no need for much, except commitment, discipline, and a willingness to teach your child the value of saving and investing.

I was speaking to Cody Travis about another book when he asked me what else I had written. Now, I'm particularly fond of *A Pizza the Action* and *50 Hidden Gems of Greater Western New York* (*Hamburger Dreams* wasn't even published yet), but what struck Cody most was *From Cradle to Retirement.*

Cody immediately saw how that book could have a compelling – and imminently more practical – sequel. That sequel is this book: *The Parent's Guide to Turning Your Teen Into a Millionaire.* He was so motivated he even came up with the cover design!

As I began the process to produce this book, Jack Towarnicky continued to encourage me and promote the Child IRA idea whenever he could. (Jack wrote the forward for *From Cradle to Retirement.*)

Along the way I ran into Jamie Hammond, Producer of PBS' *BizKid$*. Business had brought her to Rochester and gave me a chance to interview her for an article I was writing for Forbes.com. During that chat, the teen IRA concept came up. Seeing how this complimented her own work (showcasing child-entrepreneurs), she graciously accepted my invitation to her to write the Foreword to this book.

As we got close to the intended publication date to coincide with tax season – March 2020 – the coronavirus hit. Everything stopped. Everyone was sheltering in place. No one was buying anything. As a result, we suspended our schedule. Like a lot of things in 2020, this book didn't happen.

Which brings us to Pankaj Runthala. Pankaj did a masterful job prepping the print manuscript for ebook publication. This will be my first ebook. I'm thinking I might convert my previous works into ebook format. What do you think?

I want to thank my children – Cesidia, Catarina, and Peter – for offering themselves as lab rats in this grand financial experiment. Mind you, I was sort of late to the game when it came to starting IRAs for them (they were in their mid-to-late teens). Thankfully, as those who read *From Cradle to Retirement* know, there's a way to catch up. I'm happy to report that now, in the early-to-mid-twenties, my kids are on track.

Finally, and this cannot be overstated enough, none of this – any of my writing – would not be possible were it not for my wife and soulmate Betsy. She proofs all my books (and many of my articles). She finds lots of mistakes which I dutifully correct. Of course, every once in a while, I go beyond the corrections and do a little rewriting without telling her. You can tell where that occurs because that's where you'll find a typo or two.

I sincerely hope you find *The Parent's Guide to Turning Your Teen Into a Millionaire* not only entertaining reading, but an investment the yields multiple returns (maybe a million?). Enjoy the book and be sure to check out ChildIRA.com for exciting updates (and maybe even offer your own testimonial).

Christopher Carosa
Mendon, New York
January 15, 2021

INTRODUCTION:
HOW I BECAME A MILLIONAIRE IN BARELY MORE
THAN A DECADE

I t only took me a dozen years to become a millionaire.

Here's how I did it.

At age 24, my company began offering a 401(k) plan. I put away a little money into it as soon as I could. I saved at most (and this was only in the last few years) about $70 a week. Then, in 1996, I stopped contributing. Cold turkey. Before my 36th birthday.

I didn't have an IRA, let alone a Child IRA. I was already a teenager when Congress passed the Employee Retirement Income Security Act of 1974.

"ERISA" – the short-hand term for the Act – allowed wage earners to take a tax deduction for money saved in an Individual Retirement Account ("IRA"). At the time, the most you could put in an IRA was $1,500. By the time I graduated from college, the max had been raised to $2,000. It stayed at that level through all the years I contributed to my company 401(k) plan.

You needed to save more money than $2,000 a year if you wanted to retire in comfort. It didn't take a rocket scientist to figure it out. As a trained astrophysicist, I can say that with some certainty. Or you can ask my brother-in-law. He reached the same conclusion. He's had a very similar experience with his orphan 401(k) account. Oh, and did I mention? He's a working rocket scientist.

So, the 401(k) plan was the way to go. Not the IRA. Especially not the Child IRA. Remember, when I started, I wasn't a child anymore.

My experience, however, mimics the Child IRA concept: you save for a limited number of years, stop, and then do nothing. Today, that long abandoned 401(k) account is worth more than a million dollars.

In fact, it's on the same growth curve as the Child IRAs I've described here in *The Parent's Guide to Turning Their Teenager into a Millionaire* (as well as in my earlier book *From Cradle to Retirement: The Child IRA – How to Start a Newborn on the Road to Comfortable Retirement While Still in a*

Cozy Cradle.) I expect my old 401(k) account to be well north of $2 million when I begin to withdraw from it in another dozen years.

Amazing, huh? A couple of million dollars from only twelve years of contributions.

I did this despite waiting until after I graduated from college to begin saving for retirement. I did this despite no longer contributing to my 401(k) account after only a dozen years. I did this despite the terrible equity returns in the new millennium's first decade when we saw two market crashes and no growth in the leading stock indices.

Now, I know what you're thinking. "Chris," you're saying, "you must have made a lot of contributions in those first twelve years."

Truth be told, my highest salary in those years was roughly $60K. At its peak, my base contribution level was just $3,600. That's not too much. That being said, due to employer matching and a rather large bonus, in that last year I contributed close to $10K into my 401(k).

What did that get me?

All it did was it allowed me to catch-up to all those years I missed by not starting a Child IRA.

So you see, even though I never had a Child IRA, my 401(k) account ended up on the same track as a Child IRA.

A dozen years. A million dollars.

Sounds pretty straight-forward, right? Sounds easy, right?

It's even easier for your teenager.

SECTION ONE:

– THE DREAM –

YES, IT REALLY IS THIS EASY TO ACHIEVE!

Chapter 1:
How to Turn Your Teen Into a Millionaire Before High School Graduation

I'm going to cut to the quick because I want to immediately satisfy you. You bought this book for one reason and one reason only. You want to turn your teenager into a millionaire.

It's incredibly easy. Too easy. So easy many don't believe it.

Believe me, it's true. As you no doubt can guess from my own experience, (and from the experiences of many of the people I have interviewed), I've seen this idea work. I've had more than a front row seat. I've been in the game.

And you can, too. Your teenager can be a player. Your teenager can win.

The Parent's Guide to Turning Your Teen Into a Millionaire presents a simple idea. But let me warn you: be mindful of The Rule of The Entrepreneur.

There's one blunt difference between successful entrepreneurs and everyone else. Everybody – you, your neighbors, the teenager packing your grocery bag – everybody has ideas. Big ideas. Small ideas. Great ideas. Practical ideas.

How many times have you or someone you know ever heard a news story about an innovative idea only to comment, "That's nothing! I thought of that years ago."?

The difference between a successful entrepreneur and everybody else comes down to one word: implementation.

You don't reap the benefits of *thinking* how to build a better mousetrap. You can only capture those rewards by actually *building* (and *promoting* and *selling*) that better mousetrap.

The same is true with the specific Child IRA strategy I am about to share with you.

Bear the following in mind. The Child IRA is amazing and everyone can (and should) do it. Yet, too many people fail to take advantage of it. It's far too tempting to "put it off until tomorrow."

This procrastination applies to parents and children alike.

Please promise me this: Don't be one of these people. I ask that once you finish reading the last page of *The Parent's Guide to Turning Your Teen Into a Millionaire*, you and your teenager make a pledge to actually start a Child IRA.

Here's How You Begin

You know that money your teenager earns while working? Go to your favorite bank, broker, or mutual fund and use those earnings to start a Child IRA. A Child IRA is just like any other IRA except it's for a minor child (that means a parent or guardian needs to sign the paperwork).

Here's something you may not realize. Like an employer who matches an employees' 401(k) contribution, you can match the amount your child contributes to a Child IRA. Many parents and grandparents actually do this (just as long as the total annual IRA contribution doesn't exceed the teenager's earnings that year).

Now, Here's How to Turn Your Teenager into a Millionaire

Beginning at age 13, the teenager earns at least $6,000 a year (it's not a hard as you might think). Contribute $6,000 to the teenager's Child IRA. Rinse, lather, and repeat until the teenager's first year of college (or through age 18).

Then do nothing.

Add nothing more and let that Child IRA grow until the child reaches retirement age (70 years old, which it likely will be by the time your teenager retires).

Wait. I'm going to throw you a curve ball. I'm going to assume your teenager's Child IRA grows at a much slower rate than the historical average. Let's say, for whatever reason, it grows at 2-3% less than what is reasonable to expect it to grow.

What's the value of this teenager's Child IRA at age 70?

Brace yourself: It's nearly 2½ million dollars! All accomplished before high school graduation!

That's the power of compounding. That's the opportunity too many miss.

Don't miss it.

*   *   *   *   *

That's the idea. The Child IRA. It's amazing (or "big" or "small" or "great" or "practical" or whatever adjective you wish to use).

The idea is only the easy part. The remainder of the book will lay out the details needed to implement it.

But first – Spoiler Alert! – the Child IRA gives your teenager something of value that's not measured in dollars. Do you know what it is? If not, read the next chapter before proceeding.

CHAPTER 2:
EVERY PARENT'S WISH

If you're like most parents, you want to help your children. You want them to avoid making the same mistakes you've made. You want to give them an edge they can only get from experience – from your experience.

You're no different than any other parent. You want to see your children have the benefit of self-reliance at an earlier age than you did. You want them to gain the self-confidence that usually comes with self-reliance.

Why?

Because, the sooner you see your kids forge confidently ahead for themselves, the more content and relaxed your life becomes.

Hey, It's Not Your Fault!

Face it, your kids have kept you awake at night from the moment they were first born. Even adult children keep their parents awake. You've learned from the school of hard knocks how to make good decisions. You know offering this knowledge can help your children. Alas, how many kids listen to their parents?

It's natural to convince yourself there's no way your kids will ever listen to you – especially if your kids are teenagers. And if they don't listen to you, there's no way you can share the difficult lessons you've learned from your life's experiences.

That's life. There's nothing you can do about it.

Or is there?

There is a Way

Look around you. Other parents' children appear to be on the road to success.

How did they do it?

Believe it or not, you already know the answer. It lies in your response to this question: "How old were you when you started listening to your parents?" If you're like most offspring, you eventually realized your parents offered you valuable advice. You only wish you'd have listened to them earlier.

This is one of those good news/bad news sorts of things. Rest assured, at some point your kids will seek your counsel.

That's the good news.

The bad news is, like you, they'll have to relearn everything you did by attending their own school of hard knocks. The challenge, therefore, is giving them that edge you want to give them.

It's true the challenge may be insurmountable. You may not be able to give your children a head start in every endeavor. But you might be able to do it in at least one area.

Would you settle for guiding them to an opportunity that they can ignore today but will definitely be thankful for when they're your age? It's the kind of thing that they'll look back on and say to themselves, "Boy! Am I glad my parents did that for me. I might not have understood or appreciated it then, but I sure do now!"

Of course, if you took a moment to reflect on it, you'd have wished your own parents had the foresight to do this for you.

Yes, Obstacles Will Stand in Your Way

Too many outside influences draw your kids away from your good counsel. Hollywood brainwashes them to distrust you. Schools train them to think independently, but without the common-sense guidelines life has taught you. Their peers convince them they are invincible. Heck, by the time you get a chance to talk to them, society has swayed your kids to believe anything you tell them "is holding them back."

So, go ahead. Tell them the one thing they can do right now that will guarantee to make them more comfortable later in life. You know what it is. It's not an opinion. You've seen it work (at least) in others' lives and (hopefully) in your own life.

Tell them 'til your blue in the face. Chances are, unless you start well before they're inundated by these outside influencers, they'll ignore you. Just like every child ignores every parent.

Worry Not! No Mountain Can Stop You!

If you focus on the one thing you can control, you can set the seeds that will grow to become a powerful force in your child's favor.

How powerful?

Consider this: kids, from an early age, like to win. They all dream of being the best player on the team. Adolescence amplifies this very natural, very human, desire.

Now, life is filled with many different types of games. When we're young, those games are mostly physical. As we grow older, though, our "games" become increasingly fiscal.

And it's not just expensive looking goods from clothes to computers to cars. Sure, it might start out that way, but the scoreboard eventually becomes earnings and savings. Your earnings can lead to those expensive material goods, but your savings represents the ultimate measure of wealth.

When our children feel themselves wealthy, their self-esteem increases. And with self-esteem invariably comes self-confidence. And self-confidence, when correctly directed, quickly leads to success in any number of fields.

Why is this most important?

No outsider can effectively influence a child who already believes in himself. How often have you watched a self-confident child single-handedly lead the team to victory? Moreover, how many self-confident children have you seen fearlessly take on those who bully them (or their friends)? Finally, who but a self-confident child can willingly stand athwart dehumanizing peer pressure?

You can be certain of one thing. With this kind of inner strength, your kids won't be drinking someone else's Kool-Aid, they'll be pouring their own for others to drink.

What's more, they'll be doing it at a younger age than their peers. And that will make them leaders.

And when you're old, imagine how much more buoyant and cheerful you'll be knowing your kids can get by on their own. How they're prepared to help their own kids benefit from their (and, by extension, your) experience.

Now that's a legacy you can retire on.

And if your kids miss out on this opportunity. Don't worry. You can focus on your grandchildren instead. Chances are it'll be more important for them.

Why? Because, as the next chapter reveals, while we can't predict the future, we do know the future likely won't include something we all take for granted right now.

SECTION TWO:

– THE CHILD IRA –

THE BASIC IDEA EXPLAINED

CHAPTER 3.
FREE YOUR CHILD FROM
THE SHACKLES OF SOCIAL SECURITY

Another year and another dire report. Each year, the Social Security Board of Trustees releases its annual report on the long-term financial status of the Social Security Trust Funds. Like most Americans, you read these headlines. Like most Americans, you're concerned what they might mean to your retirement.

Like most parents, you're concerned what this means to your child's retirement. More important, you wonder if there's anything you can do to protect your child from the inevitable collapse of Social Security.

The good news is you can.

The bad news is time is running out. Social Security remains on a countdown clock to insolvency.

For several years now, the Social Security Board of Trustees have projected the Old-Age and Survivors Insurance Trust Fund will become depleted in 2034. This "OASI" Trust Fund is the part that pays those Social Security checks the government has promised to pay since the 1930s.

"Ouch," says every person who is retired or has ever thought of retiring.

Yes, "ouch" would be an appropriate reaction.

Does this mean the checks will stop? No. Beyond 2034, workers will continue to pay into the Social Security system. And those payments can (and will) go directly to pay retirees.

Unfortunately, the money current workers pay into Social Security won't be enough. Those payments will only be able to cover 77% of the expected payouts.

In case you're wondering, that's an instant 23% pay cut for all those receiving Social Security checks in 2034 and forever after. Thus, we can see the end of the road the proverbial can has so often been kicked down.

Optimists say Washington will bend to the political winds and tap the toe to the tin can once again.

Pessimists say all is lost.

Realists? Well realists will keep on reading. They know full well there exists an alternative to this "Blanche DuBois" philosophy that has sustained – some might say "questionable" – enthusiasm for our pay-as-you-go Social Security system. (For those too young to remember, Blanche DuBois was the character in Tennessee Williams' 1947 Pulitzer Prize-winning play *A Streetcar Named Desire*. In the play's closing scene, as they wheeled her away to the mental institution, she infamously said, "Whoever you are, I have always depended on the kindness of strangers.")

Just as Blanche didn't know where she was going, no one knows for sure where Social Security is going. What do you do when you don't know for sure? You prepare for the worst. That's the most reasonable thing to do. That is the approach of the realist.

Be a realist.

If you're not sure whether Social Security will be there when it's your teenager's turn, what can you do right now to prepare your teenager for the worst? Is there a better way?

Before we can possess this better way, there's another use the parent must first tackle.

Chuck Underwood is a pioneer in generational study and host of the television series *America's Generations With Chuck Underwood* on PBS. **He says we can't name a generation** until the oldest of the age cohort has been out of college for several years. Therefore, despite the "Gen-Z" headlines, we don't have an official name for that group of App-Affixed Adolescents currently roaming high school halls.

Nameless or not, they're part of this Social Security game just like all other generations. To say they may never know what Social Security is (or was) may be a very real thing. This, in fact, is likely to be the generation that never needs Social Security—but only if they're taught to be proactive in a way earlier generations either couldn't be taught or weren't taught.

Clearly the App Generation (there, I just gave them a name) has a tremendous benefit in time. It's a magnitude more than all other generations. Any kind of savings plan will go a long way to eliminating any need they might have for Social Security. "The more that can be saved as early as possible, the better," says John Madison, a Personal Financial Counselor at Dayspring Financial Ministry in Ashland, Virginia.

Of course, the drawback to a standard savings program is that it's too easy to get the money out prior to retirement. Even custodial trust accounts eventually revert to the minor once they reach the age of maturity. The best way to ensure the savings are locked up until retirement is to put that savings into a Child IRA. Rich Donnelly, Regional Director at EP Wealth Advisors in San Diego, says the use of this type of savings vehicles "can give children a running start towards retirement."

To free your child from the shackles of Social Security, you must first free your child from the natural impulse of spending. This isn't merely frivolous spending, it's all spending.

That's what the Child IRA achieves. For if the money is taken out, it loses much of that power of compounding your teenager needs to avoid depending on the kindness of strangers in government to keep issuing those Social Security checks.

Here's how it works.

Many teenagers find jobs as soon as they can. They want to earn money to buy things. Maybe apparel and video games when they're younger, cars and jewelry when they're older. That's the spending urge I was talking about. Use it to your (and your teenagers') advantage. If it motivates your teen to find a job, encourage your teen to work. The first requirement to starting a Child IRA is for the teenager to have earned income.

Ideally, and for the purposes of our discussion, that earned income needs to be at least $6,000 per year. As we'll discuss later, this is not a difficult goal. It's important to reach this goal because contributions to a Child IRA have restrictions. Your teenager (or anyone else) cannot contribute more than the amount of income earned for the contribution year. If your teenager only earned $2,000 last year, your teenager (or anyone else) can only contribute $2,000 to your teenager's Child IRA for last year.

There's an upper limit, too. Your teenager (or anyone else) can contribute up to a maximum of $6,000 per tax year into your teen's Child IRA.

Did you catch what I did? Did you see I kept repeating "or anyone else"? Anyone (parent, grandparent, aunt, uncle, godfather, godmother, etc…) can (indirectly) contribute to your teenager's Child IRA, so long as the total contributions do not exceed $6,000 or the income your teen earned for the tax year of the contribution. The contributor does not have to be related to your teenager.

This represents an important work-around to the spending incentive. Technically, these "contributions" are gifts given directly to your teenager. They can be birthday gifts, confirmation gifts, bar mitzvah gifts, bat mitzvah gifts, or any other kind of gift. This allows your teenager to spend some or all of the income earned.

Now, I know I said some nasty things about spending earlier, but it is a reality. Learning how to spend stands out as one of the mileposts on the road to financial maturity. As important as it is to wean your teen off of Social Security, it's just as important to your teen to discover the joys of budgeting, frugality, and making informed purchasing decisions. You can't accomplish this without spending.

Still, the bottom-line is to contribute $6,000 per year into your teenager's Child IRA. If spending needs to be cut to do this, then spending needs to be cut. (By the way, cutting spending is another important lesson.)

Now, are you listening? Here's the beauty of the plan. In nearly all cases, current laws state you can't begin withdrawing from an IRA until your reach age 59½ without incurring major penalties. This discourages spending. Furthermore, if you think your teenager might qualify for college financial aid, current eligibility algorithms shield your child's retirement assets (that would include your teenagers Child IRA). A Child IRA not only encourages saving, it discourages spending. What parent doesn't appreciate that combination?

Allowing the Child IRA to grow to its fullest, in effect, replaces Social Security. By contributing $6,000 a year beginning at age 13 and through age 18, your teenager's Child IRA will have grown to almost $2½ million at the retirement age of 70 (the "real" retirement age by the time today's kids get there).

This figure assumes an annual growth rate of 8% per year. That's 3% below the historical rate of 11%. That gives your teenager a lot of wiggle room to make some investment mistakes.

That means, by contributing $6,000 a year from age 13 until high school graduation (a total of $36,000 in contributions), your teenager has a $2½ million head start on retirement. That's on top of any other retirement savings that person might have. Where is the need for Social Security?

What a head start it is!

The Child IRA. It's that easy. It's the answer to all our retirement woes. It obviates the need for Social Security (at least that part that deals with retirement). Would you like to see how?

By age 70, when the child retires, assuming an average annual return of 8% (versus the historic average annual return for equities of 11%), the Child IRA would be worth $2,407,918. Upon retirement, your teenager takes out 4% from the Child IRA each year. That's equal to more than $104,000.

Currently, the average Social Security paycheck is $1,461. That's about $17,500 per year. Let's assume an average cost of living increase of 3% (that compares to an average of 2% for that last ten years). When today's 13-year-olds retire at age 70, the average annual Social Security payout would be less that what's they'd get from their Child IRA.

Who knows? We may discover the Child IRA is the easiest way to solve the Social Security conundrum once and for all (check our Appendix II – "The Solution to the Inevitable Collapse of Social Security" for more on this).

One more thing. The above Social Security projections assume Social Security will still be around and paying out at today's rates.

Are you willing to place your child at that risk? What are you willing to do to avoid this risk?

Let's talk about what we could do now, by ourselves, without the need for legislation, regulatory approval, or any other third-party action, to rescue your teenager from the unknowns of Social Security. Let's dive into the Child IRA as it is today. And, believe me, you're going to want to read this because it really is as easy to do as what I just described – and just as lucrative for your children (and grandchildren).

CHAPTER 4.

THE TINY SACRIFICE THAT WILL PRACTICALLY GUARANTEE YOUR CHILD RETIRES A MILLIONAIRE

I s it possible to eat healthy (and possibly lose weight) and achieve financial independence at the same time?

Do you regularly go out to dinner (at a real restaurant, not a fast food joint) with your special someone? If so, according to Zagat's you're probably spending about $40 a person (for a total of $80 a dinner).[1] Got a family, you say? Perhaps, in your busy schedule, you find it necessary to have your family meal at that aforementioned fast-food joint (that's about $5 a head for a total of $20 a meal for a family of four). Still not striking any chords with you? How about that daily Frappuccino frenzy (about $3 a cup)?

But I digress. We're here to talk finance, not food. When thinking about retirement, people have two overriding fears: outliving their retirement savings and outlasting Social Security. If they're that worried about themselves, think how worried they'd be if they consider their children's (or grandchildren's) retirement prospects.

What if I told you there was a way to easily brush aside these fears for those children? What if I told you the solution doesn't involve fancy products, fly-by-night salesmen, or too-good-to-be-true promotional pitches. Would you be interested to discover how people are already doing it? Well, it's all laid out in the next several chapters. What I'm talking about is the Child IRA. Chapter 5 ("Everything You Need to Know About the Child IRA... and Why You've Never Head of This Before"), offers a quick recap of the concept and why it's beginning to turn a lot of heads.

The great thing about the Child IRA is people don't need to change service providers to take advantage of it. It's not a proprietary product. It doesn't require large minimum investments. In fact, it's not just as easy to start as a regular run-of-the-mill IRA, it is a regular run-of-the-mill IRA!

With one key difference, however: It's started by and for someone below the age of 18. Well below the age of 18. Ideally at the age of "fresh out of the oven." Although there are a number of variations to this theme. This book gives you the game plan for one of those scenarios: using the Child IRA to turn your teenager into a millionaire.

The basic idea is this: Contribute $6,000 a year from age 13 until the child's nineteenth birthday and that modest investment will grow to two-and-a-half million dollars by the time that child retires at age 70.

Not bad, eh? Now, I know what you're thinking: If this is such a great idea, why isn't everyone doing it? Well, there are two very good reasons why we don't see Child IRAs blossoming in mutual fund accounts all across this land. First, not many people know about the Child IRA. Second, and more important, even if people are aware of the Child IRA, they aren't currently eligible to participate.

Aye, there's the rub. In order to set up the Child IRA, the child needs to have earned income. That might be easy for most teenagers, but it's harder for 13-year-olds and it's nigh impossible for teenagers in some states with the most restrictive child labor laws. How can these teens get a paying job? Fortunately, the wonderful world of capitalism provides reasonable access to a quick fix to this dilemma. Just turn on your favorite television show (or YouTube video channel) and, if you wait long enough, the answer will reveal itself.

As explained in Chapter 6 ("How to Take Advantage of the Child IRA Under Current Laws"), there is one job a child can do from very nearly the moment he is born: model. (Baby models appear in display ads and video commercials.) While the pay scale varies by market, it's not unreasonable to expect a diligent and ambitious teenager to make at least the requisite $6,000 (and much more) a year needed to contribute to the Child IRA. Job opportunities in top-tier markets often feature the added benefit of residuals, meaning the child can earn income in future years based on work done in a past year.

While modeling for third parties is quite competitive and demanding, there is a large market where it would be quite effortless for children to model for: their family's business. As long as parents and grandparents pay reasonable wages and stay within the applicable child labor laws, they can hire their own children to model for their business marketing materials. When children grow older, they can assume more traditional duties, as outlined in Chapter 7 ("Who is Using the Child IRA Right Now… and Why It Matters Now More Than Ever").

Naturally, a working child can generate more expenses that may offset any income. As luck would have it, the IRS only requires gross income to qualify for an IRA contribution, not net income. Therefore, even if the child's job may create an isolated negative cash flow situation, the parents' working arrangements still should net a hefty positive cash flow, making room to use the child's income to contribute to the Child IRA.

If that means making sacrifices, be mindful such sacrifices aren't too burdensome.

For example: $1,000 a year is equivalent to a fast-food meal for a family of four once a week; $2,000 a year is equivalent to two Frappuccinos a day; and $3,000 a year is equivalent to three dinner for two at a fancy restaurant a month.

That's only a start, but it's a big start. Remember, you're only footing part of the bill. Your teenager needs to take responsibility for a portion of it, too.

Who'd have thought you could eat healthier and possibly lose weight at the same time you're helping your child gain financial independence at retirement. If all this talk about food is making you hungry to learn more about the Child IRA, the next few pages will satisfy that hunger.

Are you afraid you're too late to take advantage of the Child IRA? Those who have this edition of the book receive several Bonus Chapters. One of these provides a detailed "catch-up" scenario you can try right now. You'll find it in the Bonus Section of this book (Chapter 19: "What to Do if You Missed the Child IRA Train? It's Not Too Late to Give a College Graduation Gift Worth $3 Million").

But, again, for those most curious, let's first recap the origin story of the Child IRA because it may be relevant for your teenager's younger siblings.

CHAPTER 5.

EVERYTHING YOU NEED TO KNOW ABOUT THE CHILD IRA... AND WHY YOU'VE NEVER HEARD OF THIS BEFORE

Beginning in the winter of 2014, a series of articles came out that represent the beginnings of a concept called "The Child IRA." The following chapters will answer the most asked questions about the Child IRA. First, I'll briefly explain the numbers behind what makes the Child IRA so attractive and some variations that allow it to be replicated. (For those more inclined, Chapter 9 – "Yes! It Really Is This Simple! or... How the Numbers Work" – takes you deeper into how the numbers work.) Next, we'll explore what's required to create and contribute to the Child IRA under current laws, including why those variations may be more realistic than the original concept of contributing $1,000 a year for nineteen years. Finally, we'll review some real-world examples of the Child IRA in action, including a twist that you might have overlooked.

Summary of The Child IRA

The genesis of the Child IRA began with the article "What Every 401(k) Plan Sponsor and Fiduciary Should Disclose to Employees: How to Retire a Millionaire (Hint: It's Easier Than You Think)," (*FiduciaryNews.com*, February 25, 2014). This piece discussed an approach commonly used in 401(k) education sessions to persuade employees to begin saving as early as possible.

The method compares a 15-year-old saving $1,000 a year for sixteen years vs. a 40-year-old saving $5,000 for the same time period. Assuming they each retire at age 70, the younger saver finds he has nearly three-quarters of a million dollars while the older saver has only a little more than half a million dollars. This despite the 40-year-old saves five times more than the 15-year-old.

A spreadsheet accident led to a follow-up article and the first recorded mention of the phrase "The Child IRA." In the course of running the numbers of the first article, the age was inadvertently reset to zero instead of fifteen.

The almost penicillin-like serendipity led to the publication of the article "This idea will solve the retirement crisis, guaranteed!?" (*BenefitsPro*, February 26, 2014). By dialing back the start age from "age 15" to "new born baby" and investing that $1,000 annually until said baby reaches age 19, we find the value of the Child IRA will have grown to two-and-a-quarter million dollars at retirement.

That's right.

For the price of a $19,000 investment, the "child" in the Child IRA becomes a multi-millionaire when retirement hits at age 70.

Said another way, for about the cost of dinner for two each month, or the cost of a family meal at McDonald's once a week, or less than the cost of that daily Vanilla Bean Crème Frappuccino at Starbucks, parents can help set their child on the path to a quite comfortable retirement. (But if you remembered what you read in the previous chapter you'd already know this. By the way, this is the point of the repetition you see repeatedly in this section of the book.)

With that in mind, it quickly became apparent The Child IRA could easily obviate the need for Social Security. The article "It's time we create a Child IRA," (*Benefit Selling*, April 2014) explains, in numerical detail, how the Child IRA can become a viable national policy to eventually replace Social Security.

Finally, the entire notion of the Child IRA was fleshed out and repurposed to become Appendix V in the book *Hey! What's My Number? – How to Improve The Odds You Will Retire in Comfort*, (by Christopher Carosa, Pandamensional Solutions, 2014). But, enough of the history lesson. What you really want to know is "What makes the Child IRA tick?"

*   *   *   *   *

About the Assumptions Used with the Child IRA

The first major assumption is the return assumption used in the 70-year period encompassing the Child IRA.

The number used is 8%.

This is roughly 3% less than the 11.20% median return for the nineteen 70-year rolling periods from 1928 through 2018 (based on the Stern-NYU annual return data for the S&P 500). Moreover, the assumed return of 8% is more than 2% less than the worst performing 70-year rolling period (10.40%).

This cushion is more than enough to incorporate account fees, timing of cash flows, and sequence of return risk.

Despite the conservative nature of the return assumption, it's best to view the $2.25 million end result as a good "approximation." It's also important to remember this retirement fund does not include retirement savings made by the child during their working adult years. Like the teenage version of the Child IRA (which yields slightly more than the new born baby version), the Child IRA is a great "head start."

The second major assumption deals with the $1,000 annual contribution. This begins from the year the baby is born and ends when that child turns nineteen. There are two important considerations with this assumption.

First, in the real world, given the opportunity most would maximize the annual contribution ($6,000 as of 2019) and not limit themselves to only a fraction of that. The $1,000 annual contribution used in our example is meant to show how easy it would be to establish and maintain the Child IRA. In addition, it demonstrates how a small sacrifice (one Frappuccino a day) can yield a return of huge magnitude (to the tune of two-and-a-quarter million).

As we'll learn in the next chapter, several obstacles stand in the way before one can take advantage of the Child IRA. For one, it applies only to new born babies. With frowns on their faces, upon hearing this parent will lamentably say, "My kids are older. Can they also avail themselves of the Child IRA?"

The quick answer is "yes."

This is the benefit of not relying on the maximum available contribution. Teenagers can "catch-up" for missed years by increasing their annual Child IRA contribution. The prequel to this book *From Cradle to Retirement: The Child IRA – How to Start a Newborn on the Road to Comfortable Retirement While Still in a Cozy Cradle* (Pandamensional Solutions, Inc, 2018) shows how to accomplish this for children of all ages. In this book, *The Parent's Guide to Turning Your Teen Into a Millionaire*, as the title states, we narrow this down to a single age group.

But it is the subtitle of this book that makes it different from its predecessor: *"And How To Do It Before High School Graduation!"*

By saving the maximum allowance contribution each year from age 13 through age 18, your teen can surpass the original Child IRA amount by almost half a million dollars. (For those living in states where teens must be 14 before they can start working, missing that first year contribution will be costly. Even without it, though, their Child IRA will still finish a tad under $2 million at that same 8% average annual return rate.)

The Child IRA for College Aged Children?

The Child IRA also works for college aged children, (although by that age, the Child IRA is nothing more than a regular IRA). We won't dwell too much on this because the circumstances have been addressed many times before as justification for starting an IRA. For the purposes of comparative continuity, however, we'll share with you the numbers in terms of achieving the same results as the Child IRA. For example, to reap the same $2.25 million reward as the Child IRA, a 19-year who begins saving $6,000 a year must contribute that same amount through age 28 then contribute another $3,500 at age 29. If the college student waits until age 22 to start, maximum contributions must be made every year until age 36, then another $2,000 must be made at age 37.

At the very least, the Child IRA for college aged children validates the power of compounding. But we're looking at starting the Child IRA when children are teenagers. There are many ways for teens to earn an income. Unfortunately, the rules tend to constrain 13-years-olds. The next chapter gives you a quick summary of one of the best – and often overlooked – options for these teens.

CHAPTER 6.

How to Take Advantage of the Child IRA Under Current Tax Laws

N ow that you know everything you need to know about the concept of the Child IRA, let's learn what it takes to benefit from The Child IRA. Remember, the one significant drawback of the Child IRA is that, under current laws, it can't be utilized unless the child has earned income. Since the full value of the Child IRA for your teen assumes IRA contributions begin at age 13, it requires your teen to have a job at age 13. Therein lies the challenge.

It's not that your 13-year-old doesn't have the skills to work. To be honest, when it comes to all things technology, the typical 13-year-old can run circles around adults. No, the problem isn't with your child. The problem resides solely in the hands of the government.

In all but a handful of cases, state and federal laws prohibit children from working until they reach the age of 14. Even then, the numbers of hours they work are strictly limited until age 16.

What's your 13-year-old to do?

Well, there's a solution hiding in plain sight right before your very eyes. It's staring right at you. Or, rather, if you're watching TV, reading a newspaper, or surfing the web, you're staring right at it.

The Best Way For Teens to Begin Using the Child IRA

You've seen commercials on TV, ads in newspapers, and pop-up pitches on the internet. What's the one thing most of them contain? People. And plenty of those people are kids, including teenagers.

For many, landing a job as a modeling professional or performance artist seems far-fetched, if not impossible. Certainly, they think, such positions are available only to those with connections, not for the common folk. Just like any other job, it's not as hard to get if you're willing to do what's necessary.

"Breaking into the business is not difficult at all," says Kent Friel, Executive Director at the Mary Therese Friel Modeling Agency in Mendon, New York. "A parent interested in getting their child into modeling should research potential agencies and look for a reputable company with a proven track record to get involved with. An agency like ours will help guide you through the process and help you learn the business."

What precisely does it mean to be a model and what are the kinds of jobs one can expect when modeling?

"The type of modeling work we are discussing here is commercial print work and television commercials," says Friel. "Typically, models in these types of bookings are seen in advertising images placed in print publications, on television, and in electronic media. There is other modeling work available like fashion/runway and television/film acting. They all have different payment rates associated with them."

How Much Can a Child Model Expect to Earn?

The first step is landing the gig. Next, the child must earn enough to start contributing to a Child IRA. Getting the actual job is only the first hurdle. Your child needs to earn enough money to cover the $6,000 annual contribution of The Child IRA.

Is it reasonable to expect the child to earn the minimum necessary to continually fund The Child IRA?

Friel says, "The question is difficult to answer because the range of compensation for child models is varied. Every booking is different, every client is different, and every model is different. Like any job, compensation rates are tied to qualifications, in many cases. The more training and experience a model has, the higher the rate they can command on a booking. Additionally, compensation for a modeling booking tends to increase based on the geographical area that an ad will be shown in (local, regional, national, etc.). This factor is usually in line with the size of the company producing the ad."

Friel divides the modeling market into three geographic tiers. "In a third-tier market like Rochester, New York," says Friel, "a child can earn approximately $50 - $150 per hour, or $500 to $1000 per day. Most of the work is local and regional in scale. Because the child model is working in their hometown, parents have the added advantage of preserving the child's normal schedule and do not have to travel for auditions and bookings."

Based on Friels estimates, a teen modeling in a small market like Rochester might need to work 5-10 hours a month or 6-12 days per year. This amount of work should generate the income necessary to sustain an annual Child IRA contribution of $6,000.

Larger markets offer higher paydays. This makes it easier to earn $6,000.

"Second-tier markets like Chicago, Philadelphia and Miami offer much regional and national work for models," says Friel. "This work pays a higher rate for the job than the third-tier markets. Top-tier markets like New York City and Los Angeles offer national bookings for network TV and pay the best rates. Models receive a standard appearance fee for the shoot and a residual fee based on the amount of air time the commercial receives. These commercials would be for national brands. Sustaining ongoing work of this nature requires joining a union (SAG/AFTRA) and being able to either travel to these cities on a regular basis, or relocate."

Can a Teenager Sustain a Modeling Career?

Let's say the choice is made to rely on a modeling career to fund the annual $6,000 Child IRA contribution through age 18. To do this, your teenager must find enough modeling jobs to produce at least that much income for six consecutive years.

Is it reasonable to expect a child's modeling career to last that long? After all, someone who's cute as a thirteen-year-old might not make the cut as body changes progress through adolescence.

"At our agency, we represent professional models from infancy through the senior years," says Friel. "We have been in business for 30 years and have models still working with us today who started their modeling careers with us when they were children. Theoretically, a person could begin modeling as a newborn and continue through all of their growing years and into their adult years."

But it's more than natural looks and talent that keep child models employed. Friel says, "This is a job that you have to possess a drive and determination to be involved in for the long term. It looks easy to observers, because it is supposed to appear that way. The reality is that much training, preparation, and auditioning happens before any work is booked. The work is truly fun and rewarding."

More important, a successful child modeling career requires a support group well beyond the child's ability to control and manage. "To be successful," says Friel, "child models need representation, professional photos, and training. They also need a parent or guardian who has the time to accompany the child to all of their modeling activities."

In short, a child's modeling career may last only so long for any number of reasons. Friel says, "Modeling careers for children end because one or more of these ingredients is missing. For example, an agency will represent a model for as long as they deem that the model is marketable, which means that the model has the physical attributes and professional acumen that the agency desires. If a model doesn't have photos that accurately show their current look, it is impossible for an agent to promote them for opportunities. As the child model ages, if they don't seek training opportunities, they won't develop the necessary skill base they need for the business."

While the actual working years may be limited, the earning years can be extended if the jobs entail residuals. Depending on the nature of the work, these residuals can last for years, allowing the child to continue to contribute to the Child IRA long after the working days have finished.

[N.B.: Chapter 12 in *From Cradle to Retirement: The Child IRA* takes a deeper look at child modeling and child acting, and some of the pitfalls of taking this route, including one very famous one.

Special Case: The Parents Own a Business

The modeling profession is highly competitive. It requires a lot of dedication and hard work to sustain a career. But there may be a way to cut corners. Parents (and grandparents, other family members, and family friends) who own businesses and actively advertise represent a special situation. In this situation, maintaining a steady stream of child modeling work may demand less rigor. "A parent of a child model can provide regular and predictable bookings for the model in the advertising that they produce for their own company," says Friel. "This situation also provides control over the child's modeling career as well, which is completely absent when the model is working for other companies."

Still, it's important for the parents to continue to do things by the book. This includes not only offering fair compensation that is justified by the amount of work completed, but also to stay within the confines of any applicable child labor laws. For example, Friel says, "In New York State it is important to run bookings like this through a professional agency, like ours, with the proper permits to maintain compliance with the Department of Labor Child Performer laws."

Are You Interested in Utilizing the Child IRA This Way?

Current or prospective parents and grandparents may be interested in looking into child modeling as a way for their children and grandchildren to generate the earnings necessary to take advantage of the Child IRA. How would they go about doing this? "Take the time to do your own research to find a reputable agency that you can trust," says Friel. "Expect to pay for your own expenses (photos, training, etc.). There is a lot of information available that says models do not need to pay for anything. The reality is that if you don't pay for them on your own, the agency will assign the cost to your 'book' and you will end up paying for these expenses, plus interest, from your bookings, or at the end of your contract if the expenses were not earned."

Not everyone is cut out to be a model. More people don't even see this as a realistic option. They instead chose a more traditional route. The next chapter provides a few examples of how they did (and maybe how you can do it, too).

CHAPTER 7.
WHO IS USING THE CHILD IRA RIGHT NOW… AND WHY IT MATTERS NOW MORE THAN EVER

The previous chapter discussed one way to fund the Child IRA. The good news, we learned the most obvious way (once you realize it) for children to earn income no matter what their age. "Under the age of 5," says Ira Smilovitz, Enrolled Agent and owner of Glenwood Tax Services in Leonia, New Jersey, "the typical job is as a child actor/model. Earnings can be anything from a few hundred dollars to many thousands."

The bad news: we also learned this ideal approach requires much advance planning and almost immediate action. For many, we are well past this stage in the child's life. Rest assured, though, mentioned earlier, children well into their elementary school – let alone teenage – years can still avail themselves to the Child IRA.

Gearing Up: Pre-Teen "Training" Opportunities

While state child labor laws may prohibit this, federal child labor law does allow parents to hire their own children (contingent, of course, on the nature of the job and the business). You should always check with a competent attorney about these matters should you have any questions.

Once you've verified you're in compliance with all pertinent child labor laws, opportunities can emerge at very young ages. Saul Simon, financial advisor with Lincoln Financial and President of Simon Financial Group in Edison, New Jersey says, depending on the child's age, employment opportunities can range from "pictures for marketing promotion, filing, cleaning, and sweeping." Besides using the income to fund a Child IRA, getting a job helps the child by "teaching responsibility and money values," says Simon.

Once a child moves from celebrating kindergarten graduation and heads into the pre-teen years, we start to see more traditional work become available. Rocky Lalvani, Enrolled Agent and Financial Coach located in the Harrisburg, Pennsylvania Area says regarding the ages between 6 and 12, "at the upper end of this would be babysitting, yard work, and other household chores. They could also help setting up technology. Because of their age the wages will naturally be very low."

Be warned, however, since paying children for working around the house may garner the attention of regulators. "The children's ages can vary and their duties and pay will vary accordingly," says Sean Moore, President of SMART College Funding in Boca Raton, Florida. "The pay needs to be commensurate with the work performed, and both must be reasonable. Paying your 8-year old $30 per hour to take out the trash not only sets unreasonable expectations about the value of a dollar, it may also raise eyebrows at the IRS. While small children will probably get paid at or near minimum wage, older kids may prove to be far more valuable to the company and paid handsomely."

Keep this in mind: an allowance is not considered earned income. Income can only be earned for actual job-related activities. In general, these do not include household chores for the family home. Again, should you have any questions, speak to an attorney familiar with the appropriate laws.

Teenage Years and a Surprise Bonus for Certain Parents Who Own a Business

Upon reaching the teen years, all those years of technological immersion – yes, that includes video games – can begin to pay off. "Most of the work is now social media driven because young kids know platforms such as Instagram, Facebook, and Snapchat better than their parents and for the cost can do a really good job in helping an owner brand their business," says Ted Jenkin, Co-CEO and Founder at oXYGen Financial in Atlanta, Georgia. "Otherwise, children are limited to mostly menial day to day labor type tasks. You must pay the kids what would be considered to be fair compensation for that job if you were to hire someone out in the open marketplace – $12 to $18 an hour depending on age and skill. The most important thing is to have the job fully documented and set up an HR file for your child."

More appropriately, rather than paying for housework, it may make more sense – and have its own set of additional advantages – for parents and grandparents who own their own businesses to hire their family descendants. "I know parents that hire their children," says Moore. "In fact, I actively recommend that business owner parents hire their children and then use some (or all) of the proceeds to fund an IRA."

Sure, earning enough money to fund a Child IRA helps the child. But, do you know hiring their child can also help the parent business owner?

Edward R. Collins, Founding Partner & Wealth Advisor at Artisan Wealth Management, LLC in Lebanon, New Jersey calls it "a dramatically underutilized tax savings strategy to hire younger family members and put them on the books. Most business owners don't realize that there is no requirement to withhold the traditional payroll taxes (FUTA, SUTA, FICA, etc.) when paying ones' own children under the age of 18, so long as the business is a sole proprietorship or a partnership in which each partner is a parent of the child. Even though this benefit goes away if the business is a corporation or includes partners who are not a parent of the child employee, almost every state allows for the child employee to be waived out of Worker's Compensation coverage if they are covered under the family medical plan of the business owner."

Besides payroll taxes, there may be income tax benefits. "Depending on the income you actually pay to the young family member, and depending on whether or not they file their own income tax return, there may be no income tax liability regardless of the funding of a retirement plan," says Collins. "Every person who files an income tax return is eligible for the Personal Exemption and the Standard Deduction."

For 2021, the Standard Deduction is $12,550. Collins suggests a strategy very appropriate for teenagers. He says, "They often do part-time work – clerical or general administrative. It needs to be at least just enough from a legitimate compensation perspective to meet the IRS earned income requirement. It is extremely important to note that taxes are a complicated animal. Before implementing any strategy, one should consult with a qualified financial professional to ensure they are coloring within the lines with the IRS."

Once the necessary income is earned, the next task is to determine which form of IRA should be used for your teenager's Child IRA. "In nearly all scenarios," says Moore, "I recommend using a Roth IRA. Because most children's income will be less than the standard deduction, the Roth IRA is a perfect fit. It allows for tax-deferred growth, tax-free withdrawals of contributions at any time, penalty free withdrawals of earnings for college expenses and tax-free withdrawals upon retirement. Some families are just starting to take advantage of this strategy while others have been doing it for 5 years or longer."

Bob Chitrathorn, Vice President of Wealth Planning/Senior at Trilogy Financial in Corona, California, agrees with Moore. He says parents "are using Roth IRA's and have been doing them for a few years."

We'll consider this issue more fully in Chapter 11 "To Roth or Not to Roth?"

In the meantime, here's something you don't want to forget. Remember, with a Child IRA, your teen only needs to earn the money. That money could be spent on other items and the actual contribution can come from any source.

"Often the parents will gift the IRA contribution," says Smilovitz. "In other words, if the child earns $1,000, the parent(s) gift $1,000 to the child to fund the Roth IRA and let the child keep the earnings to use as the child wishes (subject to parental approval)."

Real-Life Stories

What follows is a compilation of several real-life examples of the Child IRA in action. Parents and grandparents with teenagers (and even pre-teens) will find these stories very useful, especially if they own a small business.

Benjamin L. Grosz, a benefits and tax attorney at Ivins, Phillips & Barker in Washington, DC, says, "I know a business owner who hires his nieces/nephews (he has no children of his own) and has coordinated with their parents to use the funds to set up Roth IRAs for the children. They have been contributing to them for a number of years. The children were first hired when the youngest was quite young (age two, I think). They have been employed as models, and paid in line with industry norms."

"I know half a dozen – maybe more – real estate investors who do this," says Don Tepper, Owner of Solutions 3D, LLC in Fairfax, Virginia. "Most of the children are now age 10 or greater. The type of work they do includes envelope addressing, postcard addressing, stuffing letters into envelopes, applying stamps to envelopes, and sealing them. (Basically, different elements of direct mail campaigns.) The pay range is between $7-$15 per hour. They have been contributing since the child/children were old enough to perform some sort of useful work – in a few cases that I know about, around ages 6 or 7."

Of course, it's not surprising that financial advisers themselves have taken advantage of the Child IRA. "I was able to give my kids '$200,000' this past Christmas in their retirement account," says Lalvani. "I did this, making sure they had earned income and then figuring out the best retirement account to put it in. It's hard for younger kids to earn an income and if the IRS thinks it's not reasonable you may run afoul of them. Laws make it hard to work for someone else."

Smart parents are quite aware of the concept of the Child IRA. Some have known about it for a long time. Here's a testimonial from someone whose father established a Child IRA for her two decades ago. "My father did this for me when I was 12 or so," says Erin Kelley, Founder & CEO of Collizio, Inc. in Washington, DC. "I did clerical work (filing, mailing, etc.), and I was paid $7 an hour. I worked enough to maximize the contribution. We used a Roth IRA. I still have it, 20 years later, though I used some of the contributions to pay for graduate school."

Kelley exposes one of the drawbacks of using a Roth version of an IRA for a Child IRA. Since one can withdraw the original contributions from a Roth without consequences after five years, there may be a temptation to use that money to pay for expenses other than retirement.

Casey St. Henry, Financial Associate at Thrivent Financial in Ellison Bay, Wisconsin says, "I work with a number of small business owners who employ their children and use their earnings to fund a Roth IRA on the kids' behalf. They tend to choose the Roth account for the tax-free withdrawals to help fund their children's education. The folks I'm familiar with all have children in the 6 – 14 age range, and they do a number of different tasks. One of my colleagues has his five children clean the offices of his business. They go in every Sunday after church and get their work done. Another family that I work with owns a restaurant, and their three kids do everything from salad prep in the kitchen to bussing tables to hosting and working as wait staff during the slow times. I don't know their actual pay range, but all of them work pretty much year-round, and come close to maxing out their Roth accounts at $5,500 per year. *[Author's Note: Beginning in 2019, the max was raised to $6,000.]* I find that the amount of time they've been using this strategy depends on how early they have been made aware of the possibility and the risks inherent in the workplace. Many of the people I work with have low-danger businesses, so the kids can start young, doing menial tasks, without much risk of injury."

"The Child IRA" may represent a recent name for something that a few forward-thinking people have been employing for some time. It's a retirement savings tool that has been far too underutilized. Granted, regulators have not made it easy for children to start their own IRA. For instance, it might be easier if, like the popular 529 college savings account, the IRA contribution rules were changed to allow parents, grandparents, or any other adult for that matter to fund Child IRA contributions out of the donor's earnings rather than require the child to have earnings. Still, that there are a number of Child IRAs currently in existence attests to the usefulness of this idea.

In the next section, we'll begin with a much more complete story of how one family started IRAs for their children. Then we'll explore each of the areas touched in this section in much greater detail. Unlike the preceding chapters, which are meant to be an overview on The Child IRA, the following chapters contain the nuts and bolts of what you must do to establish a Child IRA.

SECTION THREE:

– THE HOWS AND WHYS –

SETTING UP A CHILD IRA FOR YOUR CHILDREN AND GRANDCHILDREN

CHAPTER 8.
SAVING YOUR FAMILY INTO WEALTH...
FOR GENERATIONS TO COME...

It was the late 1990s. The stock market was booming, riding the wave of dot-com enthusiasm. Amy Bernstein was working as an attorney for the wealth management area of Harris Bank in Chicago.

One day, while skimming through "a 'retail' magazine or website," she happened upon an article describing the benefits of setting up an IRA for a minor child. Amy discussed the idea with her husband Bob, who was a manager at the Academic Computer Center at the University of Illinois at Chicago. The two decided the article made sense.

As Amy and Bob were salaried employees working for big firms, they decided to wait until their children were old enough to work. Because neither had been operating a family business, they realized they couldn't hire their kids to do work for them and, at the time, Amy didn't want to mess around trying to document babysitting jobs.

Jennifer, their oldest, was very good with managing her day-to-day expenses. (One thing Amy and Bob did with both their kids was give them a clothing allowance in their teens.) When she was old enough to work, Jennifer got her first in a long series of typical jobs kids her age have had. She worked as a camp counselor, a grocery store cashier, and taught ice skating for the park district.

Jennifer didn't demonstrate a whole lot of enthusiasm in investing, but she understood the benefit of saving and, especially, of saving early. Despite this understanding, she never really showed an interest in managing money in terms of investments.

When that first outside income came in, Amy sat down with Jennifer to discuss the idea of establishing a Roth IRA with her teenage earnings. "I have a vague recollection of my mom telling me that she was setting up a Roth IRA for me when I was in high school," recalls Jennifer today. "My parents have always been small "C" conservative with money – they have saved first and spent second – and so the news that my mom was creating some sort of savings vehicle for me wasn't really surprising."

Jennifer let her mom do everything. "She told me what she was doing, she wanted me to be informed, but she knew if she left it up to me at age 16 it wouldn't get done – at most I might have signed some papers." So Amy opened up a Roth IRA for Jennifer at Harris Bank when she was a senior in high school from the $593 Jennifer earned that fall as a cashier and ice skating teacher.

Amy remembers, "The interest rate was a whole .79%. It stayed in the savings account until March of 2002 when I had her roll it over to Vanguard. At that time, we made a $2000 gift to her to add to the IRA, based on her earnings for 2001, which included the spring of her senior high school year (cashier and skating instructor) and summer camp counselor. At that point, it went into a money market fund (don't ask me why). I think I wanted her to get involved in investment decisions and she wasn't really interested so I just opted for something that would be safe."

Amy and Bob's son Andrew, on the other hand, had long been interested in investments. "I don't really know what got Andrew interested," says Amy. "But as you can see from Jen's story, it wasn't because she was interested in investing. Andrew, on the other hand, was interested in all things related to money."

When he was 9-years-old, Andrew got the chief investment officer of Harris Bank to invest five dollars for him. Andrew celebrated his 16th birthday in 2006 and began working (as a camp counselor, camp director and soccer coach). As part of helping him set up his own Roth IRA, Amy had the "talk" with him. "It definitely added to his already existing interest," recalls Amy, "he even opened a brokerage account when he was 18 and invested in stocks with his earnings."

From Andrew's perspective, his mother's idea fascinated him. "I remember feeling intrigued," says Andrew. "My mom explained the concept thoroughly and I understood that the money being put away now would be there for me when I retired. She explained that the money would generate interest, which meant that the money would make more money. She also made sure I understood that I shouldn't ever touch the money in my Roth IRA until retirement because I would lose out on a lot of money if I did that."

In February 2007, when Andrew was 16, Amy opened a Roth IRA for him. It was initially funded with the $349 he had earned the previous tax year. Two $1,000 contributions were added that fall. Even though Andrew earned this money, he was able to spend it on other things as his parents gifted the contributions used to fund his IRA.

Jennifer and Andrew also had jobs in college during the year and summers, including tutoring Hebrew, working as a camp counselor, working as a dorm resident advisor and working as a travel coordinator for an international youth exchange program. "I let them keep the money they earned and made the contributions myself as gifts to them and put in the maximum of eligible earned income," says Amy.

While both Jennifer and Andrew continued to contribute to their IRA through college, the two children approached their IRA differently. Jennifer let her mom handle it while Andrew took a more active role. (In addition to his IRA, he set up an E*Trade account for trading stocks and mutual funds.)

There was an additional major difference between Andrew's IRA savings and Jennifer's. Given Andrew's interest in investments, his IRA was immediately invested in a stock fund. "We put his money straight into a stock fund, the Scout International Fund which was then managed by UMB," says Amy.

Today, both of Amy and Bob's children are productive adults. Jennifer (34) and Andrew (26), are both very happy to have the nest egg.

Outside of their IRAs, Jennifer, who is a foreign service officer, is also making substantial contributions to her federal thrift savings plan account. Andrew, who teaches in a charter school in Memphis and seems to work more than 24 hours a day, has a small 401(k), in addition to his state pension plan.

Amy says, "I attribute their saving for retirement on their own in employer sponsored programs to the fact that they have seen the benefits of investing at a young age through their IRAs, plus the example my husband and I have set, putting aside the maximum allowable for retirement over the years." Though both of their children have good jobs,

Amy and Bob still make annual gifts to them to cover at least part of their retirement savings.

Now, nearly twenty years after first discovering the benefits of establishing the IRAs for the children, the entire family sees the benefit and is glad to have done it. Her husband credits Amy with driving the whole idea from the outset. "Amy is way better at recognizing and acting on issues like this proactively," says Bob. "She is really, really good at taking a conservative, long-term approach to financial planning and acting on it. Not just IRAs for the kids, but our own pensions, savings for colleges, investing in a house, and so forth."

While pleased with heeding the advice of that article she read two decades ago, in retrospect, Amy does have a couple regrets. "I think," she says, "I would have tried to find a way to document babysitting jobs, etc… before they turned sixteen to start the Roth IRAs sooner." In addition, at least in terms of Jennifer's IRA, Amy wishes she had invested for the long-term rather than safety. "I should have been in stocks for her right from the start," she says, "but given her lack of interest and my conservatism, we missed a significant opportunity along the way. That being said, at least the money was saved!"

For Jennifer, the experience has been both beneficial and eye-opening. "I don't think I totally grasped the benefit of having a Roth IRA started before I personally could afford to pay into it because I've never been hugely fascinated by finances," she says. "I think a general understanding is necessary but I'm fiscally risk-averse and I'm not drawn to investing. But I got the concept of compound interest so it sounded like a good (and generous) idea. Now, understanding more about savings and finances, it's an even better and more generous idea. My family tends to live long (a grandfather died at 99 and my other grandfather will turn 99 this December) so the amount of money I'll need to save will be considerable, which can only happen through compound interest over decades."

Andrew, the more aggressive investor, seems delighted with the way things have turned out. "I've learned that the earlier you start saving, the higher returns you will have over the course of 30-40 years," he says. "It also piqued my interest in other investment vehicles. I love having a retirement vehicle that typically generates a healthy return every year. I feel secure in knowing that I have over $20,000 in a Roth IRA at the age of 26 that will provide a nest egg for when I retire in addition to my teachers pension and other savings. I feel fortunate that my mom had the foresight to set it up for me and contribute over the years."

Amy continues to be proactive, only now it's on behalf of others. "I have been preaching setting up Roth IRAs for kids to lots of people," she says. "They find it interesting, but I don't think anyone has done it. I'm not sure if it is because they don't have the excess cash or it just seems too strange. You do have to have confidence that your kids won't take it out when it is under their control, just like if you use an UTMA account."

While Jennifer hasn't yet had the opportunity to share the good news of her experience "because I'm not asked," she isn't afraid to offer it. "I think parents most often talk to other parents about child issues, and finances are always a tricky topic for Americans to discuss," she says, "But I would if asked."

Andrew, on the other hand, appears to have been put in the position of being asked plenty of times. "I have fielded a lot of questions from friends about financial planning," he says. "My advice is always the same: once you build up a savings account that covers 4-6 months of expenses open a Roth IRA. Take care of the immediate, then the long term, then invest in medium term."

As for the future, there's no question about it, Andrew would do the same thing for his children what his mother and father did for him. The school teacher says, "The benefits of starting to invest money that will yield interest for 50+ years is the smartest thing you can do for your kids besides paying high property taxes for access to excellent teachers and saving for college so your kids can graduate debt free."

CHAPTER 9.
YES! IT REALLY IS THIS SIMPLE! OR...
HOW THE NUMBERS WORK

Remember when you were a little kid and you fell and you scraped your knee? It hurt bad and it seemed like the pain would never go away. If you were really young you probably cried and cried. Pitying you, your mother would come up to you, give you a loving hug, and say, "Yes, I know it hurts now, but the pain will eventually go away." And, you know what? Your mother was right.

Time may heal all wounds, but it does something else. The passage of time insulates us from our worst fears. One of the greatest fears we innately possess is the fear of the future. Well, it's not exactly a fear of the future, it is the fear associated with uncertainty, the fear of the unknown.

Let me give you an example. After more than three decades (or more if you count my teenage ventures) of business and entrepreneurial experience, I can look back and confidently say, "That was easy." With the benefit of the rearview mirror, I can clearly see how all the dots are connected.

Building a sustaining business – no matter what market that business caters to – seems to me a straightforward process. Even looking ahead in planning the future, the benefit of this veteran template allows me to reduce uncertainty dramatically.

(People often say I'm not afraid of risk because I've started so many businesses from scratch. I tell them the truth is quite the opposite. I am risk-averse. Before I begin a new project, I try to identify and mitigate as many risk factors as possible.)

With this mindset in mind, I got to thinking. I figured if I could consistently build sustainable businesses, anybody else could. All they needed was a variation of the template I've been using. So, I approached my daughter, a recent college graduate, with the idea. It wasn't for her, as she has a career track in mind. It was more for her peers. When I suggested people her age didn't need to worry, they just needed to follow this template, her response hit me like a slap in the face.

"Dad," she said, "you're looking at this with the benefit of hindsight. You see a road behind you that you have already travelled. People my age see a road ahead, and they have no way of knowing what's coming around the bend."

Uncertainty. It's not the fear of the future, it's the fear of the uncertainty that comes with the future. The future represents a fork with many roads to choose from. And above this fork of many roads hovers the ominous cloud of uncertainty. Which is the best road to take? Not even Robert Frost can give you the correct answer.

In fact, the farther ahead you look, the darker that cloud of uncertainty becomes. When we talk of the Child IRA, we're talking about a time span of 60, maybe even 70 or 80 years. Yes, eight decades is a very long time, but remember, time heals all wounds.

In this case, it's not wounds we seek to heal, but uncertainty we wish to reduce. Long time frames accomplish this by smoothing an otherwise bumpy road. We see this with the average annual return of stocks. From 1926 through 2018, the median annual one-year return for stocks is 13.70%. That doesn't mean every year produces this same return. That time period includes 93 individual one-year returns. These returns ranged from a gain of 53.99% (in 1933) to a loss of 43.34% (in 1931). Lest you think these wild swings are limited to the Depression era, the post-World War II data is just as volatile. The biggest gain was 52.62% (in 1954) and the largest loss was 37.00% (in 2008). That's a lot of uncertainty!

Let's see how time heals this "wound" of uncertainty. The time span from 1929 through 2018 contains 23 70-year periods. The median average annual 70-year return was 11.20% The best average annual 70-year return was a gain of 11.92% while the worst average annual 70-year return was a gain of 10.40%. That's a spread of only 1.52% among all the 70-year returns versus a spread of 97.35% for the one-year data. See how time reduces uncertainty? (The professionals call it "time diversification.")

In fact, the graph below represents the highest, median, and lowest average annual return for rolling time periods from 1926 through 2018. It clearly shows a reduction in the uncertainty of annual returns as you extend the time span from years to decades.

This graph also shows us something else, and it's rather interesting. The average median return for all the rolling periods is 10.96%. Look at the solid line on the graph. This represents the median average annual return for each rolling time period. See how remarkably flat it is?

Now, truth be told, we can't use past market performance to predict future market performance. Why? Because the future is uncertain. That being said, the future has always been uncertain, and yet, we witnessed an average annual return on U.S. stocks of 11% from 1926 through 2018.

A lot of bad stuff happened during those ninety-one years. We've had multiple severe recessions, a Great Depression, a World War, a Cold War (and countless other wars), hurricanes, earthquakes, and any number of natural and man-made disasters. Do you think people didn't live in uncertainty back in the day? Your reaction might mimic my "in-hindsight-business-template" feeling, but, and you can ask anyone old enough to remember living through these events, there were definitely times when people wondered if there would even be a tomorrow.

Average Annual Returns for Rolling Time Periods
(U.S. Stocks – 1926-2018)

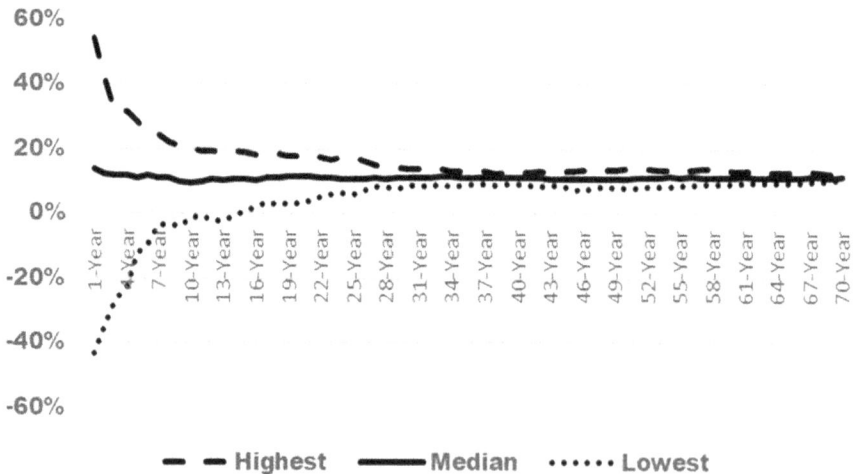

What will the world be like in 70 years when today's newborn babies retire? Who knows? What will the market return be over that time period? Who knows? Intuition suggests, however, that the world will be a better place and the average annual market return over that time period will be 11%. Intuition isn't much, but at least it gives us a basis for going forward.

You might therefore ask, "If the average annual return is 11%, why don't we use that number rather than the 8% in our Child IRA assumptions? Well, in a word, "uncertainty." Recall my answer to those who told me I wasn't afraid of risk. I'm risk-averse. My figuring is this: Between inflation, fees, and bad luck, that 3% haircut ought to account for most of the things likely to erode returns.

For the record, after contributing $6,000 a year from age 13 until your teenager reaches birthday number 19, the 8% annual return assumption used here produces a value of $2,407,918 by the time said baby (née "child," now adult) retires at age 70. If we used the average annual return of 10.96%, that value at age 70 would be $10,585,258. Not bad for 57 years (i.e., starting at age 13 and retiring at age 70.)

Incidentally, this number ranges from $3,716,899 if you were unlucky enough to begin the Child IRA during the worst performing 57-year period (8.86%) to $39,559,519 if the stars aligned just right and you began your Child IRA during the best performing 57-year period (13.66%). All of the sudden that $2½ million sounds like chicken feed.

Before you get too excited about those eight-digit home-run numbers, keep in mind the raw average annual return numbers probably include some factor for inflation. That's because stocks are generally considered a hedge against inflation. In order words, stock prices tend to go up as inflation goes up. Another way to think of this is, seventy years from now, $10 million might be only worth what $2 million is worth today. So, those home-runs might need to have an asterisk by them since they have been juiced up by inflation.

But you can't hit the ball if you don't swing the bat. Before you start spending these imaginary millions, you need to get the ball rolling and establish that Child IRA for your teenager. The next chapter tells you something about the Child IRA you may not have realized. It's not a show-stopper, but neither is it the IRA you're used to.

CHAPTER 10.
NOT YOUR FATHER'S IRA – HOW TO OPEN A NEW CHILD IRA FOR YOUR CHILD OR GRANDCHILD

If you're like most Americans who have IRAs, you're familiar with how easy it is to set them up. Simply go to your friendly neighborhood bank, broker, or mutual fund, sign on the dotted line and – Bingo! – you're done. You have an IRA and it's ready to start accepting your annual contribution.

The Child IRA, while still an IRA, isn't quite that easy. It's not hard, but it's not that easy. You caught a glimpse of this in Amy Bernstein's creation of IRAs for her children.

By the way, Amy referenced something she read in the 1990s about establishing IRAs for teenage children. Indeed, for many years the concept of a "child IRA" referred to either adult children saving for retirement or getting teenage children started on the road to retirement saving.

The experience of the Bernstein family shows how this is done. It's possible the article that inspired her might have been found in *Kiplinger's 1999 Tax-Saving Guide.* This was a special supplement to *USA Weekend* distributed to participating newspapers nationwide on Sunday, March 14, 1999. At its peak, Gannett's *USA Weekend* was the second largest Sunday magazine and distributed through more than 800 newspapers.[1]

Kiplinger's 1999 Tax Saving Guide contained the article "Make Your Child a Millionaire." The article begins "How would you like to teach your children an invaluable, double-edged lesson about tax planning and long-term investing? Oh, and set them on the road to being millionaires at the same time?" It details how a 16-year-old who sets up an IRA and then contributes $2,000 for just three consecutive years will end up with $1,111,000 when that teenager retires at age 67. Kiplinger's example assumes the 11% annual return based on the data we showed in the previous chapter.

The article was brief (about 600 words) and didn't go into much detail. Still, this idea of targeting teenager workers as potential IRA contributors has been a prominent marketing strategy of financial advisers for quite some time (and still is today).

As a typical example, there's this paragraph under the heading "When children enter the working world" from a column called "Financial Focus," written by two brokers in Carlinville, Illinois for their local paper:

> *"Encourage IRA contributions – An Individual Retirement Account (IRA) is a great retirement savings vehicle. As long as your children have earned income, they may contribute to an IRA, so you may want to help them max out on their contributions each year. While you can't directly contribute to a child's IRA, you can write a check to your child and encourage him or her to use it for funding an IRA."[2]*

So, where do you go to set up a Child IRA? "Most companies don't have IRA fees anymore, so most major discount or online brokerage houses will do this," says Jenkin. "It's likely they won't give you advice. So, you either go that route or you have an advisor who will include the account in the overall family accounts or do the work pro bono."

In January 2016, Fidelity introduced a specific program geared towards teenage IRAs. Called "Fidelity Roth IRA for Kids,"[3] the well-regarded mutual fund company made a concerted effort (and continues to do so) to educate families on the benefits of having their high school children establish IRAs.

"When we launched the product, we did outreach and marketing online, in our branches, and direct mailing – emails and letters – to customers about the product," says Maura Cassidy, vice president of retirement, Fidelity. "Our representatives may also suggest the product to customers as they have planning sessions with those customers. We also try to get the word out via media outlets like yours that people should consider saving in a Roth for Kids."

Financial service firms often incorporate teenage IRA education into their standard IRA literacy materials. While targeting different age groups, both use the same retirement saving vehicle – the IRA. Like any other IRA, a Child IRA can only accept contributions based on the earned income of the owner (in this case, the child). Cassidy says that income "could be from a job at a family business or as a model/actor, as suggested; other jobs could be paid internships or summer jobs." These jobs can be as mundane as "babysitting or mowing lawns."[4]

This is what makes the Child IRA so rare, especially among younger children. "The child has to have income to be eligible for the account, plus the child would need to not spend this money. This is not a common practice among your average family," says Christine Russell, Senior Manager, Retirement and Annuities at TD Ameritrade. "With that said, it is not unusual in the retirement industry, especially among children of the wealthy."

While the earned income requirement might seem an obvious obstacle, less apparent is the technical twist required when opening up an IRA for a minor child. "When an individual establishes an IRA, he or she is entering into a contract with the financial institution sponsoring the IRA," says Timothy Stokes, a spokesman for Vanguard. "Due to restrictions on the ability of a minor to enter into a valid contract, Vanguard IRA documentation must be signed by a custodian, who must also be listed on the account. IRAs for minors cannot be opened online. Once a minor reaches the age of maturity for their state of residence, he or she can request the 'A Minor' designation be removed."

According to Fidelity, "Minors cannot generally open brokerage accounts in their own name until they are 18, so a Roth IRA for Kids requires an adult to serve as custodian. The custodian maintains control of the child's Roth IRA, including decisions about contributions, investments, and distributions. In addition, statements are sent to the custodian.

However, the minor remains the beneficial account owner and the funds in the account must be used for the benefit of the minor. When the minor reaches a certain required age, typically either 18 or 21 in most states, the assets must be transferred to a new account in his/her name. Once the minor reaches age 21, he/she can request a transfer of the assets to his/her own independently owned account."[5]

While opening a "Custodial" or "Minor" IRA sounds complicated, it's really no different that the custodial accounts parents have been setting up for their minor children for years. "We use TD Ameritrade as our custodian," says Marianela Collado, CEO and Senior Financial Advisor with Tobias Financial Advisors in Plantation, Florida. "I can't speak to any other custodian, but it would be important to work with an adviser who works with a custodian that offers a free trade platform so that the earnings don't get consumed with fees. That is super important."

"It is straightforward: An IRA application is completed and signed," says Russell. "Some IRA vendors will not accept minor IRAs as a business policy, but at TDAmeritrade we do and are happy to open the account. Requirements are: The minor IRA has one Account Owner (the minor) and one Custodian. The Custodian signs the application, oversees and operates the account, and must be the parent or legal guardian. Minors have to be below the age of majority for his/her state, not just below 18."

The Nuts and Bolts for Establishing a Child IRA: An Example

Anyone below the age of 18 must use a "custodial" IRA to establish a Child IRA. They cannot set their own IRA until their 18th birthday. This doesn't prevent them from establishing an IRA as a minor, they just need to have a custodian do it for them. Once a child reaches the age of maturity (between 18 and 21 depending on the state), the custodial IRA must revert to the "child" (now adult) owner, and the custodian duties are formally terminated.

Things get a bit dicey with the age requirements. For example, if the child's birthday is on February 6th, and they want to establish an IRA the year they turn 18 for earnings they made the previous year (when they were 17), there are two different scenarios. First, if the IRA is established before February 6th (i.e., before the child's 18th birthday), then it must be a custodial IRA. Second, if the IRA is established on February 6th or later (i.e., on or after the child's 18th birthday), then it must be a standard IRA.

This brings up an interesting question. What happens if a custodial IRA is established when the child is, say, ten-years old. Now, the strange thing about this child is, although he lives in Denver, Colorado, he's a big Buffalo Bills fan.

Actually, it's not so strange. His family moved to the Mile High City from Buffalo when he was in kindergarten. He celebrates his 18th birthday and is showered with Bills jerseys, caps, and a signed Doug Flutie poster (don't ask why). He's old enough now that he can (heaven forbid) immediately go on eBay and sell those items.

Oddly, though, he can't assume the full rights to his Child IRA. Why? Because the age of maturity in Colorado is 21. That means he needs to wait another three years before he can transfer the IRA to his full ownership.

On the other hand, had his family never moved away from Buffalo, he would have had the opportunity to take full control of his IRA on his 18th birthday. The age of majority in New York, as it is in all but four other states (Alabama, Colorado, Mississippi, and Nebraska) at the time of this writing, is 18 years.

What does this all mean for your teenager?

Once it's determined your teen has earned income, establishing a Child IRA isn't too difficult.

Go into the office of your favorite financial services firm and ask for a "Custodial IRA Application" (it may also be called a "Minor Child IRA" or "IRA for a Minor Child" application). Bear in mind, some institutions do not provide for these types of IRAs, but most major banks, brokerage firms, and mutual fund companies do (you can access Fidelity's application on-line). Also, there may be a minimum deposit required to open the account.

Here's a real-life example of what you might see.

A recent visit to the local Schwab office yielded a form called the "Schwab Custodial IRA Application." This four-page application appears very similar to a standard custodial account application. You'll need to complete information (including name, address and Social Security Number) for both the teenager as well as the custodian. Only the custodian is required to sign the application.

The first question many people ask is "Who should be the custodian of the Child IRA?" The custodian can be any adult, but it's most commonly the parent or grandparent. Aunts, Uncles, other members of the family, and even close family friends can also serve as custodians. It's a good idea to identify and indicate who the successor custodian will be in case the assigned custodian can no longer fulfill the duties.

Once the paperwork is completed, signed by the custodian, and handed to (in this case) Schwab along with Schwab's required minimum deposit of $100 – and *voilà!* – your teenager now has a Child IRA (technically a "Custodial IRA" to use Schwab's terminology).

Ah, yes, as simple as pie, except for the fact we overlooked an important "first" decision. Before you set up the Child IRA, you need to decide whether it will be a Roth or a traditional IRA? Don't know the difference? Don't know the advantages and disadvantages of each? The answers lie ahead in the next chapter.

CHAPTER 11.
TO ROTH OR NOT TO ROTH?

Whether it's mowing the lawn or babysitting, minor children can place earned income into a Child IRA. The question is: Which one? The traditional IRA or the Roth IRA?
For some of you, the better question is: What's the difference?

The traditional IRA was created under ERISA in 1974. It allowed you to make a $1,500 tax-deductible contribution to an Individual Retirement Account ("IRA") as a means of encouraging more people to save for their own retirement and rely less on corporate pension plans. The maximum contribution was raised to $2,000 in 1981. Since then the limit has gone up regularly to where it is today (2019) – $6,000 per person with an addition $1,000 "catch-up" allowance for people age 50 and older.

The traditional IRA, while offering a tax break at the beginning and permitting tax-free growth, contained one stipulation: when you withdraw money after age 59½, you had to finally pay taxes on it. After a couple of decades of this, people started to think it might make sense to add a "pay me now" alternative to this already existing "pay me later" option. To answer this need, in 1997 Congress created the Roth IRA.

The Roth IRA is treated exactly the same as a traditional IRA save for two very important differences. First, the bad news: There is no tax deduction associated with contributing to a Roth IRA. Second, (we can't have bad news without some counterbalancing good news), you pay no taxes on any withdrawals after age 59½ (as long as you wait five years after contributing to the Roth before withdrawing).

"In terms of flexibility of withdrawals (i.e. availability to pull from the account before age 59½ without penalty) the Roth IRA will give the owner the ability to withdraw the contributions to the account on a tax-free and penalty-free basis after the contribution has been in the account for at least 5 years," says Alex Vaccarella, a financial planner at AEPG Wealth

Strategies in Warren, New Jersey. "There are no exemptions for the investment growth on those contributions, however. As an example, if I am working and manage to put away $10k into my Roth over two years (say, $5k at age 15, $5k at age 16) I will be able to withdraw $5k tax and penalty free from the account when I turn 20, and by the time I am 21 I will be able to pull the full $10k in contributions. Assuming I earned 5% per year on that money, my account balance should be in excess of $13k when I turn 21, so I'll be left with $3k+ in the Roth after I pull my $10k in contributions."

The basic difference, then, between a traditional IRA and a Roth IRA is this: A traditional IRA is a tax-deferred (i.e., "pay the government later") retirement savings vehicle while a Roth IRA is an after-tax (i.e., "pay the government now") retirement savings vehicle. The differences can be important considerations when determined which flavor of IRA to choose when opening a Child IRA.

So, what are the most important factors parents need to consider? Financial planner Charles C. Scott, founder of Pelleton Capital Management and co-creator of FinancialChoicesMatter.com in Scottsdale, Arizona, says, "The key is whether a tax deduction matters or not. The traditional IRA is deductible, the Roth IRA is not.

Clearly, the specifics of one's tax situation represents the highest priority item when deciding whether to open a traditional IRA or a Roth IRA. "The biggest difference is the taxation," says Derek Hagen, Founder of Fireside Financial LLC in Minneapolis, Minnesota. "Deposits into a traditional IRA are made pretax (meaning you get a deduction on your current year's taxes), but then you have to pay tax on the withdrawals. Deposits into a Roth IRA are made after tax (meaning you do not get a deduction), but you don't have to pay taxes on the withdrawals. So, the difference really comes down to whether you think you will have a lower tax rate now or in the future."

Think about this for a moment. It is the child who must earn the money that is placed into the Child IRA. Is it likely the child will earn as much as an adult? "The most significant difference between traditional and Roth IRAs is when the saver will be taxed," says Jason J. Howell, President of Jason Howell Company in Vienna, Virginia. "High income earners, unlike a child, can benefit from a tax break today. Typically, someone who intends to make more money later in life may benefit from paying taxes today (and not tomorrow)."

While how and when taxes are applied may be the first main difference between the Roth and the traditional IRA, there is another difference. "The second main difference is when the money can be withdrawn," says Zach Stuppy, President of Brave Boat Capital Advisors located in Boston, Massachusetts. "For basic distributions, the distribution age is 59½ for both IRA types. However, the Roth IRA offers some flexibility for early withdrawal. You can take penalty free, early withdrawals from a Roth to pay for education expenses or for a first-time home purchase (with limitations). A Roth also allows for the return of principal without penalty."

It's not just "when" you can take the money out, it's also when you "must" take the money out. "The traditional IRA grows tax deferred but you pay tax when the money is withdrawn in 50+ years," says Michael Landsberg, a Partner at Landsberg Bennett Private Wealth Management in Punta Gorda, Florida. Unlike the traditional IRA, which requires distributions to begin no later than age 70½, Landsberg points out "the Roth grows tax free and there is no tax or mandatory distribution at age 70½."

With these factors in mind, is one type of IRA better than the other when it comes to establishing a Child IRA? Financial advisers from across the nation are generally of one mind on this.

"Unless the child's income puts them into 25% or more marginal tax bracket, ROTH! ROTH! ROTH!" says Ilene Davis. "Why give up potential tax-free future income to get a 10-15% tax deduction. If the child does a good job saving through life, tax bracket in retirement should be higher."

It's a straightforward calculation. "With minor children, under normal circumstances, I think it is always better to use a Roth IRA," says Vern Sumnicht, CEO/Founder of iSectors® LLC & Sumnicht & Associates LL in Appleton, Wisconsin. "As long as the minor has earned income, up to $6,000 a year can be contributed to a Roth IRA. Those dollars will grow tax free for the minor child for a long time."

The "pay taxes now" appeal of the Roth is quite apparent given the tax circumstances of most children. "The Roth IRA is hands down the better choice in this situation," says Scott Vance, Enrolled Agent at Taxvanta in Cary, North Carolina. "The Roth is contributed after-tax, but is not taxed when taken out. A traditional IRA is a tax deduction when a contribution is made but upon withdrawal it is taxed as ordinary income. So, in the case of a child, using a traditional would provide rather small deductions since generally when children are minors their income level is low as is their tax rate. The Roth would not provide that rather small deduction now but many years down the road in retirement the Roth would be withdrawn tax free, during a period when the tax rates are projected to be higher thereby providing a much better overall deal."

Simply stated, the tax-deferred advantage of the traditional IRA does not exist for most children. This is truer now as the 2017 Tax Cut and Jobs Act increased the standard deduction to $12,000. In other words, anyone making $12,000 or less per year (think your teenager) won't have to pay any federal taxes.

"When it comes to minor children, the Roth IRA wins out every time," says Ken Hoyt, of Hoyt Wealth Management in Westford, Massachusetts. "Here's why: Roth IRAs offer no immediate tax benefit, but they grow completely tax-free if withdrawn after age 59½. Minor children typically are in the lowest possible tax bracket, or pay no taxes at all; however, they will always assuredly be in a higher tax bracket later in life. Conversely, a traditional IRA offers an immediate tax benefit which the minor child will not realize."

"Minor children don't need the deduction, so the Roth will always be the better choice," says Scott. "Having to pay income tax on a small amount of money today and not ever having to pay it again makes way more sense. Roths grow tax-free and the money comes out tax-free. There are some rules for the Roth that limit the tax-free withdrawal feature, namely that a Roth account (not all Roth accounts) needs to be open for a minimum of 5 years, after which the contributions can be taken out without tax. Also, the tax-free feature on the growth inside the Roth only happens after the owner is 59½ or older. These are 'retirement' accounts after all."

With a Roth IRA, it's very possible your teenager will never pay taxes on earnings and the growth of those earnings. "A Roth IRA is better in almost all instances," says Stuppy. "The minor is contributing after tax dollars to the IRA and with most minors earning so little they would be in a very low tax bracket or pay 0%. Therefore, no taxes would be owed up front and any distributions would be tax-free. This leads to a situation where the minor could potentially never pay taxes on these assets. The withdrawal flexibility a Roth IRA offers also makes it a better choice in almost all scenarios. This flexibility allows the money to be withdrawn early for a number of reasons and thus it isn't tied up until the minor turns 59½."

Because the child's tax bracket is usually very low, it even makes sense to pay those small taxes now in exchange for avoiding higher taxes in the future. "In general, we recommend using the Roth IRA," says Ben Westerman, Senior Vice President at HM Capital Management in St. Louis, Missouri. "Even if the parent ends up paying a little bit of the child's tax (via the "kiddie tax"), as long as the parent can afford and wants to pay the tax, the Roth IRA is the way to go."

Hagen agrees. He says, "A Roth is best when you are currently in a low tax bracket. Pay the tax when the rates are lowest. By using this for children with earned income, they will never have to pay taxes on the account again (as long as they hold the account for at least 5 years before withdrawing)."

Is there ever a time when it might make sense to use a traditional IRA as the preferred vehicle for a Child IRA? Yes, but those times are very rare and very narrowly defined. "There are very few instances when a traditional IRA makes sense for a minor," says Stuppy. "Most minors make such little money that they will owe no or very minimal taxes so the upfront tax savings of a traditional IRA would be negligble. The only instance that it may make sense is if the minor makes a high level of earnings. In this case, the traditional IRA would help to offset the tax burden."

Still, there may be advantages to showing no after-tax income, regardless of how small it is. "I guess the only area where a traditional IRA would make sense for a child would be in the case of a child who earns a lot of money and is in need of ways to reduce their adjusted gross income ("AGI") to become eligible for some credits or deductions," says Vance.

Besides a large income and qualifying for other benefits (like college financial aid), traditional IRAs do offer additional perks not found in a Roth IRA. Landsberg says, "There are also some extra abilities inside the traditional IRA to withdraw for college or a first home that the Roth does not have."

The decision may seem cut and dried, but it's always best to consult with the appropriate advisor to make sure the appropriate type of IRA is used when establishing a Child IRA. "The traditional vs Roth IRA debate is not a new one, and there are valid arguments on both sides," says Hoyt. "Traditional IRAs are clearly better when the account owner is currently in a high tax bracket but expects to be in a lower bracket when retired. The opposite is true for Roth IRAs. If someone's future tax bracket is unclear, then there is no clear advantage to either type of IRA."

There is one disadvantage a Roth IRA has compared to a traditional IRA. With a Roth IRA, you can withdraw your original contribution after five years. You don't need a reason. You can use it for anything. It can provide the necessary funds for a down payment on a house. It can help pay for a college education – even graduate school! Of course, if you don't need a reason, that means you can withdraw the funds for less noble reasons, like buying that 80" 3-D Smart TV, purchasing not just a Mustang, but a Shelby GT350®, or ordering a… (well, you get the picture). The point is, unlike the safeguards imposed by the withdrawal restrictions of a traditional IRA, the Roth IRA requires steadfast discipline to avoid the temptation of premature withdrawal.

You're probably thinking, "But I thought early withdrawal was an advantage to the Roth?" It is, but only in the sense that there's an emergency and there is no other alternative. The problem is, once you withdraw, you lose all the advantages of decades of uninterrupted compound growth. That might be too big a price to pay for the immediate gratification of going from zero-to-60 in 4.3 seconds behind the 526 horsepower 5.2L Ti-VCT V-8 engine.

In either case, go ahead and make your decision. Then, let the contributions begin!

Oh. Wait. The child has to earn that income first. Well, as we said, that's the real hurdle in this entire enterprise. Russell says there are several typical earnings opportunities for children. She cites "family businesses (where the child is paid a wage), and child models/actors. Perhaps another group might be younger professional athletes with high income from endorsements (Olympians for example). Advisors and those in the financial services industry also open these accounts for their own children who have income, to start the children on a long-term savings path."

Yet, there other ways to allow your teen to reap the riches of the Child IRA. The next chapter reveals an easy process to help you identify what these may be for your teen.

Chapter 12.
Four Steps To Kickstart Your Teen Tycoon's Career

Most teens think of summer jobs merely as a way to earn petty cash. These ventures can offer something much more than that. They can open the way to life-long joy and riches. Here's how parents can cultivate their child's inner-entrepreneur.

Summer blossoms as that time of year when all red-blooded American teens turn their minds to making money. Sure, they might see it as the opportunity to buy the latest video game download, go to the mall, or catch the latest summer blockbuster with their friends. Of course, there's something else they can do that will give them more than they can imagine (if you haven't figured that out yet go back and read the title of this book).

First, though, they need to find a job.

But not just any job.

Traditionally, teenagers look for jobs stocking shelves, checking out customers, or cooking fast food. With higher minimum wage laws, these jobs are harder to come by. What's an enterprising young teen in search of ready cash to do?

Why not explore the many opportunities of self-made wealth forever associated with the innocence of youth? These are the proverbial lemonade stands, baby-sitting, and lawnmowing services kid entrepreneurs have been doing since, well, since teenagers have discovered the twin joys of free market capitalism and open market consumerism. Overall, it's been a win-win formula for teens, their parents. and the nation as a whole.

Summertime jobs have become a serious business for families. Teens who earn their own bacon place less financial pressure on parents. With the new tax law creating a standard deduction of $12,000, most teen workers find they'll pay no federal tax at all.

For teens relying on their own wits rather than working the usual retail jobs, the benefits of summer gigs rise significantly. They teach so many invaluable life-long lessons. Running your own business shows you how to be independent, self-confident, and well-organized.

Just as important, working for yourself educates in a manner no book can. It's hands-on learning. The teen entrepreneur quickly discovers everything from very practical financial know-how to critical decision-making skills.

How can parents encourage a child's entrepreneurial fervor? It's easy, but it's hard. It's easy in the sense you can simply rely on a child's natural curiosity to act as the divining rod. It's hard because many parents see this natural curiosity as "not practical" or "lacking in common sense."

While this parental view might be true for someone of mature age (like a parent), parents need to remember most kids will need to explore. And exploration includes venturing down blind alleys and dead ends. What might be obvious to a parent is not obvious to a child. Allow the child to fail (within reasonable limits) to both satisfy the child's curiosity and to cause the child to learn through experience.

To cultivate the child entrepreneur, it's best for parents to take a multi-step approach. This may take several years or, if the child is particularly inspired, several months. No matter how long it takes, these four steps can kickstart your teen tycoon's career.

Step #1: Explore Hobbies to Find Your Teen's Passion. Younger children should be encouraged to probe their interests and begin to develop hobbies. In their tween years, parents can start to guide their children to take the hobbies they are most passionate about and begin developing those hobbies into potential businesses. Maybe these proto-businesses won't make any money at first, but the summer provides a great opportunity to experiment because it offers more free time.

Step #2: Find a Problem to Solve. There's another approach to creating a teenage business that has proven successful. Teens often find they have unique obstacles. Overcoming these obstacles requires creativity and skill. All the better if your teen's passionate hobby also solves a personal problem.

This provides two sources of the motivation required to commit to running a successful business venture.

Step #3: Search for a Potential Audience: Teens will often find their friends have the same problem. Solving their own problem will also solve their friends' (and other teens') problem. This presents a budding profit-making opportunity.

Step #4: Slowly Test that Market: Whatever the source, treat any new business idea as a continuing experiment. "The first step is to identify a need in their community that they could fill," says Jamie Hammond, Executive Producer/Co-Creator of *BizKid$* in Seattle, Washington. "Have teenagers dips their toes in the water by gauging the interest level of their potential market. Does their audience share the enthusiasm for the same hobby? Does the same problem bug them, too?" Only when questions like these are answered can the teen test the willingness of the market to pay for the solution offered.

These four steps might sound a lot more complicated than a simple lemonade stand, but the process is identical:

- Child enjoys making lemonade (a passionate hobby)
- Child is thirsty (a personal problem)
- Child discovers other people are thirsty, too (potential audience)
- Child puts some empty cups and a pitcher of lemonade in a little red wagon, rolls the wagon to the roadside, and places a sign that says "Lemonade: $1" to see if people are willing to pay for it (starting small and testing the market).

Parents play a critical role in the development of their children. It's no different for kids who want to create their own business. "Parents can help their kids to make their budgets," says Hammond. "They can even loan their kids the first money to purchase materials to make their products or to buy the tools they might need for their service. However, paying their parents back must be part of their budget."

Every child should have the chance to start a business, even if it's really small. "Running their own business allows kids to learn that they have determination to stick to their commitment and how personally rewarding that is, no matter how much money they make," says Hammond.

The lessons learned from the experience continue to pay dividends throughout one's life. Teens may even find themselves on an easy road to becoming a millionaire before they graduate high school.

Would you like more meat on the bone of this four-step process? Read the next chapter and you'll discover seven usual, unusual, and rare teen job ideas.

Chapter 13. These Seven Summer Jobs Can Put Your Teen On the Road to a Million Dollar Retirement

As a parent, have you ever wondered how best to cultivate your teen's inner entrepreneur? Sure, you've gone through the 4-step process to help your child develop a business idea. And yet, sometimes you just need a kickstart to get those creative juices flowing.

With that in mind, how about a quick rundown of the kinds of entrepreneurial jobs teens might consider starting this summer? Not only do you have the three usual suspects, but it's not too hard to find three unusual suspects. What many, if not most, overlook, however, is the one rare suspect. Find all seven below and a bonus you simply won't believe.

Usual Suspect #1: Lemonade Stand

OK, let's stop right here with this time-honored tradition. It seems quite a few municipalities have been cracking down on these roadside ventures. The reasons range from lack of permits, to Health Department issues, to the kids being just too darn young.

It's come to such a point where New York State is considering legislation specifically permitting child operated lemonade stands. (This came about because last summer the New York State Department of Health forced a 7-year-old to close his lemonade stand.)

Who knew such a classic rite of passage now needs explicit government approval?

Still, serving food and drink does present certain issues, so it's understandable and easier (as well as prudent) to limit the "make something" category to arts and crafts. Think of the kinds of things kids assemble at summer camp. Small little knick-knacks that are cheap, easy and quick to make while also serving a useful purpose. For example, pencil holders, picture frames and kitchen magnets fall into this category.

Of the three Usual Suspects, this one requires the most financial attention. "Teens must create a budget to make sure that their income will be more than their expenses," says Hammond.

Usual Suspect #2: Baby-sitting

This represents the first of our service categories. We'll call this "passive" services. That means you don't have to necessarily do something unless the situation demands it. For example, in babysitting, if the baby is sleeping, you don't have to do anything unless the baby starts crying. Then, hopefully because you're properly trained, you'll know what to do.

When it comes to "sitting," however, think outside the box (or the baby crib). Teens get paid for house sitting and pet sitting. In fact, dog walking is a business model adopted by many people well beyond their teen years.

Whereas the first Usual Suspect emphasizes accounting smarts, the second Usual Suspect stresses reliability. "Teens must establish that they are dependable and will be responsible in delivering the service that they are offering," says Hammond.

Usual Suspect #3: Lawn Mowing

This is the "active" service category. In other words, you don't get paid for watching the paint dry, you actually have to do the painting. Landscape maintenance is a perfect example of this. Not only does this include mowing the lawn, but you will often find yourself weeding the garden, edging the grass and watering the plants.

This third Usual Suspect requires some budgeting (since you have to spend money for the equipment) and demands reliability. In addition, though, you'll also add the need for a specific skill set that matches the job. "Offering a skilled service is taking on the responsibility of knowing how to do the work and delivering a good quality job in performing that service," says Hammond.

Don't limit your active service to the outside world. This time think inside the box (or the house). You can hire yourself out to organize a neighbor's messy garage or shed. Similarly, empty nesters might want a more thorough house cleaning (to rid themselves of their now-vacated kids' old stuff).

This last job actually introduces us to an entire new list of "Unusual Suspects." Now we're stepping into terra incognito for most parents. It's also a most lucrative arena. Teens who master this domain may discover for themselves not only a summer job, but a lifetime career.

Unusual Suspect #1: Online Selling

You know all that junk you just pulled out of your neighbor's house? They might ask you to dump it in the trash can, but you might profit by remembering the saying "one man's trash is another man's treasure." There may be a market for that trash. Setting up an eBay store is one way to determine if there is.

Selling another person's "trash" could therefore bring in two paychecks for the same job: the first one for cleaning out the mess; and the second one for selling the unwanted materials collected from that mess.

Want a variation on this theme? Try combining Unusual Suspect #1 (Online Selling) with the "make something" category (Usual Suspect #1 above). You may uncover an easy way to distribute those things you make. Word of warning: Don't forget to account for the cost of postage and sales tax in your pricing strategy.

Unusual Suspect #2: Content Creation

Here you venture into the realm of the YouTube star. Of course, it's not limited to YouTube or even videos. Any type of creative content (videos, podcasts and blogs) can be distributed and monetized via the internet. This might have been easier a couple of years ago before popular platforms changed their rules, but it's still possible today.

Teens who have a hunger for entertaining and public presentation can excel in this arena. They will learn marketing techniques that will prove useful in many other fields and careers. In fact, by demonstrating acumen here, less social media conscious members of older generations may just hire you to become a…

Unusual Suspect #3: Social Media Manager

Remember the joke about the parents who had their toddler work the VCR? (For that matter, do you even remember VCRs?) Face it, when it comes to the latest technology, anyone who doesn't remember VCRs or CDs or iPods or Myspace (before it was an all-news site), qualifies as a social media expert.

Of course, that doesn't necessarily mean you are, but it's a lot easier to get your foot in the door. Having the experience managing your own content (see Unusual Suspect #2) can give you an edge. Speaking of gaining an edge, there remains one kind of summer job that will give teens the ultimate advantage. You might call it…

Rare Suspect #1: The Family Business

If you want to excel in any field, it's best to have an experienced mentor nearby to hold your hand. What better mentor than a parent? Working for the family business blends together a powerful series of tools and opportunities that can help propel the budding teenage entrepreneur to greater heights.

Parents serve as handy role models for their children. Watching mom and dad perform their jobs on a day-to-day basis shows the kids far more than any words can ever explain. When children see what their parents do as entrepreneurs, they're more likely to pick up on it.

There's an added benefit to working in the family business. Depending how it's organized, minor children working in a parent-owned business can improve family wealth. These children, besides being in lower tax brackets (remember, the first $12,000 earned falls within the standard deduction and therefore pays no federal tax), they may not have to pay payroll taxes. If the family lives in a state with no income tax, then the child pays no taxes of any kind on the first $12,000 earned. Even with state income taxes, the amount paid can be very small.

Here's an amazing bonus to all these seven types of jobs. Because of the low tax rates, these teens can retire as Child IRA multimillionaires tax-free by establishing a Roth version of the Child IRA!

Who knew you could be all set for retirement by the time you graduate from high school?

So, what are your supposed to do to take the next step? The final section of this book supplies several practical templates for you to follow depending on your specific situation.

SECTION FOUR:

– YOUR STEP-BY-STEP GUIDE –

TURN YOUR TEEN INTO A MILLIONAIRE BEFORE HIGH SCHOOL!

Chapter 14.
Gaming and Saving

Long before he was married, Rodney Davis, a systems analyst, knew what his financial priorities were. Making good money and without the financial burden of having a family, the twenty-something year old did something rarely found in that age group: He focused squarely on what he wanted, made a plan on how to get there, then carried out that plan. As with many of his generation, the foundation of that plan would have made Lucy Van Pelt (of Charlie Brown fame) proud: Real estate.

Not only did Rodney buy his family home before he had a family (indeed, before he was married), he also invested in rental properties used by full-time students at a popular state university.

Well, time went on as time tends to do. Rodney married Erica, (by coincidence, also a systems analyst), and they had three wonderful sons, Alex, Ray, and Adam. Rodney and Erica continued to work hard at their jobs. Still, they had time for their boys, activities, from sports, to scouts, to robotics. The little side business of student rental property continued, too. When the boys got old enough, like all children whose family have their own business, it was the kids turn to toil the earth (or, in this case, wax the floors).

For Rodney, bringing the kids in to work and starting their Child IRAs went hand-in-hand. "There is an old wise tale that you have to hear about something ten times before you realize that you have heard it," says Rodney. "I had read and investigated opening up a Roth IRA for my wife and myself. Unfortunately, the limitations on how much you could invest into the Roth IRA reduced the amount that we could earn. That small return wasn't enough to excite either Erica or myself to open an account."

Then, one day, came the proverbial bolt from the blue. "While glancing through the *Bottom Line* publication, I read an article about setting up Roth IRAs for your children," recalls Rodney. "The article spoke about investing $4,000 a year for 10 years (age 15-25) and along with a conservative rate of return, your children would have hundreds of thousands of dollars at retirement age. The amount would even double or triple, if your children continued to invest after age 25. The concept hit me like a bolt of lightning, especially since the oldest of my rug rats had reached 15 years of age and all my kids were helping me with property maintenance on our rental properties."

Very quickly, as you might expect from a man of action, Rodney began moving his kids – one at a time – into Roth IRAs. "I started my two oldest kids (Alex and Ray) on their Roth IRA when they were 15 years old," says Rodney. "It was a perfect combination of teaching them the value of hard work, learning a skill, and investing for the future. Surprisingly, my kids did not see the opportunity that I saw in this endeavor. They focused on the hard work part of the job: cleaning apartments, landscaping yards, and painting rooms."

Perhaps now might be a useful time to digress with a funny story that many parents whose children help them in their business might recognize as typical with their kids, too. Rodney tells the tale like this:

"My youngest child, Adam, a teenager at the time, has a story which epitomizes the hardship of hard work. Alex, my oldest son, and I had sanded down the wood floors in an apartment to prepare for a coat of polyurethane. The plan was for Alex and me to polyurethane the edges of the rooms & hallway while Adam would then spread the polyurethane across the wide-open spaces, a relatively safe and harmless job with little room of getting it wrong. That was the plan, but we all know how plans go."

"My initial mistake was not introducing Adam to polyurethane first. I had popped open a can of polyurethane and began to set up Alex to start coating the edges. Adam decided to get up close and personal with the gallon can of polyurethane. The polyurethane fumes and strong odor caused him to repulse immediately, he ran out of the apartment while screaming, 'I'm not going near that stuff.' It took me over a half hour to convince him to come back in and try."

"When we went back into the apartment, he was not ready to polyurethane the floors. I realized that he needed more time to acclimate to the task at hand. While his big brother and I started the edge work, I had him stand behind us and watch. After about a half hour, he was ready to try and coat the floor of the room."

"I took some time to show him how to apply the polyurethane with long, even brush strokes. You know, the kind of things dads all over teach their kids. He's a fast learner and quickly took to the job. Meanwhile, Alex and I were way behind schedule, and we needed to focus on completing the edge work."

"Now this is where the fun begins. Alex and I had completed the edge work in that room, so we moved on to the next room. Adam kept varnishing away, integrating his brush strokes with our edging. Little did we realize that instead of going across the room with his polyurethaning, he was going around the room in a clockwise fashion."

"A few minutes later we heard a yell from the other room, and, sure enough, he had painted himself into a circle in the middle of the room."

"Now, keep in mind, Adam is the most daring in the family. He was going to show us that he could jump from the center of the room to the doorway entrance. I had my doubts, but I didn't have a better idea at the time. He crouched down, like a tiger ready to leap upon its prey. He took one little step forwards and tried to leap. His front foot slid out from underneath him and he ended up on his butt on the newly covered polyurethane floor. To make it more of a catastrophe, he then flipped over onto his hands and feet to get off the floor. He was covered with sticky polyurethane from hands to toes."

"Needless to say, Adam did not care about his financial reward in spending money or in a Roth IRA that day."

Now that you've had your little chuckle at Adam's expense (in real life, he laughed, too), let's get back to the real story. The process of opening the Roth IRAs was a piece of cake for Rodney. "This was easy," he says, "I kept track of the hours and wages paid to my sons. They would take their payroll check to the bank, part was used for free spending (video games, etc.) and part was earmarked for savings. Once they had enough money saved up, they had a bank check drawn and filled out the brokerage form for the Roth-IRA. Voilà! They had opened their Roth IRA."

Rodney discusses money matters with his children all the time. Unlike opening the Roth IRA, that didn't start off too easy. It's dad and mom up against three typical all-American active boys. You might say Rodney didn't have a fighting chance, but that's exactly where he wanted his boys to be when the conversation started.

"When they were very young," he says, "I pushed concepts on them, saving versus spending. But investment concepts fly over the heads of children. They're more concerned about their video games and battles. So, I put investing concepts into their video game strategies. Before you can conquer the enemy, you must build your army first. One dollar represents a warrior. To build your army, you need a dividend paying stock which will create more dollars for you, which then increases the size of your army. Next, you need to train your warriors to fight and earn an upgrade. A trained warrior is stronger and more skillful, which provides a better opportunity to win. If you buy quality stocks to build your army, you are more likely to receive more dividends or earned capital gains vs. a non-quality stock which stagnates in price or doesn't increase dividends."

As they got older, the conversation relied less on the metaphor of the pixelated screen. For the Davis kids, the Child IRA came in baby steps (pun intended). "Before they opened their Roth IRAs," says Rodney, "I had opened regular brokerage accounts for them. I would discuss buying and selling stocks with them. Whenever, I come across an interesting article, I will forward the article web link to them."

They got into the groove as boys, but, as men, Alex, Ray, and Adam, can stay in the game with their father. "Now that they are adults," says Rodney, "when we talk on the phone, I will ask them 'What is new in their lives?' Remember, money doesn't buy love. Later on, at some point in the conversation, I will ask them about 'How are your investments doing?'"

Each son has developed his own personality when it comes to dealing with his IRA (and his dad). Rodney says, "My oldest son, Alex, who knows more than his father, takes an active role in decision making. For his accounts, he is the one who makes the buy and sell decisions. He and I have enjoyable conversations discussing investment strategy or how to allocate our investments for the future. He enjoys investing."

"My middle son, Ray, who knows more than his father, does not pay attention to his investments," says Rodney. "He is willing to let his father manage his investments. At this time, his focus is on his career and working long hours, so maybe things will change as he gets older or starts to raise his own family."

As he told us during his humorous story, Rodney says, "Adam, my polyurethane hero, is the risk taker in the family. He wants to chart his own course, but will listen to Dad once in a while. We'll discuss investment strategy and stocks to buy, but we don't always agree. Recently, he decided that he wanted to invest in Bitcoin, to the disagreement from his father. In the end, sometimes a teacher cannot instill the lesson to the pupil, sometimes the pupil has to learn the lesson for themselves from the School of Hard Knocks."

Speaking of the School of Hard Knocks, would Rodney have done anything differently based on what he now knows? "Life is always throwing new challenges at you," says Rodney. "With the downturn in the economy and college expenses, the Roth IRA plan for our kids was not executed as prescribed in the *Bottom Line* article (i.e., save $4,000 per year for 10 years). You cannot go back and change the past, so going forward I will strive to accomplish the Roth IRA plan for my kids (i.e., helping them save $4,000 a year for 10 years). Plus, I will continue to discuss & enlighten my kids on the value of managing their own finances & investments."

Rodney and Erica have prepared Alex, Ray, and Adam in ways no school can (perhaps other than the one involving Hard Knocks). The boys have investing experience and a financial planning perspective rarely found among their age group, or twice their age group for that matter. Therein lies the most important secret of the Child IRA. Sure, it can help your child retire in comfort, but that's not because the Child IRA grows seven digits (that's in the million-dollar range for those nodding off). The real secret behind the Child IRA is that it helps put your teen in the frame of mind that will allow your teen to make proper choices regarding saving and investing for their retirement. As a result, they'll be better prepared to retire in comfort, no matter what happens to Social Security, company pension plans, or public policy.

Establishing a Child IRA benefits the next generation. Given its tremendous power, the Child IRA remains one of the most under-appreciated retirement savings tools available. In the remaining chapters, we'll present a virtual "how-to" manual that shows how different groups of people can implement and enjoy the advantages of the IRA. Feel free to start with the chapter that best represents the group you're in, but you might discover some ideas in reading the other chapters, too.

CHAPTER 15.
FOR TEENAGERS – THESE REAL-LIFE EXAMPLES SHOW YOU HOW TO SUPER ACCELERATE YOUR WEALTH

If you're a teenager (or maybe even a "tweenager"), this section is for you. But, before we get into some of the details of what you can and should be doing, I must congratulate you. The fact that you're reading this book tells me you have what it takes to be a winner in life. Winners plan ahead. Winners have no time for people who say, "you're too young to do this." Winners take control of their own lives and don't wait for someone to give them a helping hand. And, while this book is essentially about what you could do for yourself, these very traits will no doubt be noticed by colleges, employers, and your community. These attributes represent the qualities of leaders, and every organization wants leaders. They will be wanting you.

Believe it or not, in this great big country of ours, many young people have not learned the importance of demonstrating self-confidence. But quite a few have. As you begin to reach towards more competitive goals, you'll discover many like-minded peers who show these same characteristics.

Now, if you really want to *WOW!* colleges, employers, and your community, you'll want to show something more than just a drive and ambition to achieve. You'll actually want to show a list of real, practical, accomplishments. While the Child IRA will certainly count as an impressive feat, it will be the things you need to do in order to open and contribute to a Child IRA that will be the real feather in your cap. This chapter is about those things.

Remember, to contribute to a Child IRA, you'll need to earn income. The key word here is "earn." Money given as gifts doesn't count. Interest and dividends from investments don't count. Money that you find on the street won't count, either. You will need to go out and get a job. It can be any kind of job. You could deliver newspapers. You could sell lemonade on the sidewalk. Anything.

Here's the amazing thing: you are in a unique position to discover a business – or a way of doing business – that no one else has started yet. The fact is, you have an unfair advantage. You're too young to know the barriers and obstacles that might prevent you from pursuing an idea. This might sound bad but it's not. It's good. It means you can envision a path to success in a way no adult can.

You have another advantage. You're so young that you're still impressed by ten dollars. This might sound bad, but it's not. It's good. It means you're willing to start a small-scale operation that could grow larger. In contrast, adults might look at the same opportunity and say, "Why should I go through all that trouble just for ten dollars."

The biggest advantage you have, however, is your knowledge of your customers. You know kids in a way no adult can. This definitely is a good thing. You know what bothers you, what things you'd like to have, what games you like to play. Chances are, if you want these things, so do other kids your age. If you can make or provide those things, other kids will buy them. That's a really big advantage.

And age is not a restriction. If anything, age makes it easier, because the younger you are when you start, the easier it is for you to be successful (and the younger you'll be when you start your Child IRA!). The younger you are when you start your business, the fewer kids your age will also be starting businesses. That means less competition and a greater chance at making the money you need to contribute to your Child IRA.

There's one thing for sure that bears repeating: Age is not a barrier, it's an advantage.

How do I know this? Because I've done this. I'm not just some old man using words to inspire you. I'm an old man who, as a young child, was inspired to make money. All I'm trying to do in this chapter is to share with you that same excitement I had as a kid entrepreneur.

Here's a few examples of what I did:

Towards the end of elementary school and into middle school (that's roughly the age of 11-13), my friends and I decided "kids like carnivals." So, for several days each summer for three years, we set up a carnival in our neighborhood. We made games for carnival-goers to play. We sold food we (or our mothers) made for our customers to buy. We even performed live action events for our visitors. That first year, we made seven dollars. That was a lot of baseball cards in those days. We were very excited with our success.

We figured we hit on a great idea, so the next year we added two new features. First, we included a movie presentation (we borrowed a Laurel and Hardy movie from the local library) and we converted a portion of my friend's walk-in basement into a fun house. That year we made eleven dollars. This excited us even more.

The year-over-year growth of more than 50% inspired us to extend both our offerings and our marketing efforts that third year. Rather than borrowing a movie from the library, we made a short (five minute) movie involving those little plastic army men, stop-action photography, and lots of (innocent) pyrotechnics. I was the cameraman. I was a pretty bad cameraman, but everyone got a kick out of the movie.

I was much better, however, when it came to leading the improved marketing campaign. In the first two years of the carnival, we focused only on the kids in our small neighborhood. We had a handful of much larger neighborhoods around us. That's who I marketed the carnival to in the third year.

On the opening day of the carnival, I was nervous. I didn't know if anyone from outside our neighborhood would come. Rather than sitting back and waiting, I got on my bike and rode to the neighborhoods to remind all the kids. In one of the neighborhoods, all the kids had already left for the carnival. There was about two dozen in the group. They were the first to arrive at the carnival (when I wasn't there). One of my friends who was helping with the carnival thought it would be funny to tell them the carnival was over, so those kids left and never came back. They had all this money to spend, but didn't, because somebody wanted to make a joke. It turns out that joke wasn't too funny and really hurt us.

We did have other neighborhood's kids come, and that third (and final) year we nearly doubled the previous year's take with a gross revenue of twenty-one dollars – even without those two dozen kids who came and left! This was our last year because it was evident everyone didn't approach the carnival with the same level of seriousness. This is what happens when you go into business with partners. If you're not all on the same page, if you don't all agree on the same goals, the venture will break apart.

That was OK, because I used those neighborhood contacts to start my next venture. I didn't make any money on this one, but I had a lot of fun. You see, back in those days, it was very difficult to play organized football. Sure, there was Pop Warner and Vince Lombardi football, but it was very expensive and usually inconvenient to join those leagues. Instead, we played sandlot football on our street. Kids in each neighborhood would play pick-up games in their respective neighborhoods. And that would be that.

Not quite, though. When it comes to sports, kids like to brag about their abilities. Each neighborhood would brag that it had the best team. There was no way to prove it, of course, because the neighborhoods never played against each other.

That's when I had my great idea to form a neighborhood football league. I would arrange game schedules. We'd go play at local elementary schools. Those were the only fields big enough for our teams. It was still sandlot football. This meant there were no referees – we had to learn how to play fair by ourselves. It also meant there were no parents – we had to rely on our own devices to get to and from the playing fields. Most important, it meant there was no game clock. We'd just play until dark. Our league gave each neighborhood a chance to prove its bragging rights.

I'm happy to report our neighborhood never lost a game.

But the really great business idea occurred during the era of the neighborhood football league and really blossomed into my high school years. This was the mid-1970s and sports card collecting was about to go mainstream. My brother and I anticipated this (or were just lucky with our timing) and started a baseball card/football card dealership before any kids knew the meaning of the term. This was the age when most of our peers were turning away from collecting baseball cards and moving on to other things. As a result, they were more than willing to sell their cards to us in bulk (in other words, we didn't have to pay that much money for their cards).

Still young enough to know what our peers wanted (money for their cards), we were also old enough to set up tables at adult card shows and sell our cards to both kids and adults. We soon learned how to get cards directly from the manufacturer. At its peak, this business made a few thousand dollars a year. That was more than enough for me and my brother. It also shows what happens when two partners are in total agreement with how the business should be run. Unfortunately for us, we didn't know about IRAs at that point in our life because Congress had just created the law.

My stories are decades old. The world of kid business has changed – dramatically! Today, it's easier for teens and pre-teens to start their own business. First, parents are more accepting of their kids starting businesses (since the 1980s, our country has taken on a much more entrepreneurial flavor). Second, the kids themselves are more quickly immersed into business and finance because they can see so many examples through the internet and social media (not to mention video games). Finally, again because of the internet and social media, there has never been a time of greater opportunity for kids to develop their own business. I'll end this chapter with a dozen examples of kids as young as five who have started their own businesses. Take a look at these and see if they can inspire an idea or two in your own head.

Elementary School Entrepreneurs

Ken & Kate's Snow Cones.

Shantae Pelt, Founder of Coco'Pie Clothing in Gilbert, Arizona, has two daughters who created an LLC for Ken & Kate's Snow Cones. Mikayla started the business at age 9 along with her sister Kennedy who was then five-years-old. Shantae describes the girls' venture as a "Snow Cone Business operated via a snow cone cart on wheels. They use a machine capable of crushing 500lbs of ice per hour and a variety of cane sugar syrups at the customer's choice. Each Snow Cone cost $1 and tips are highly encouraged."

The idea came to the sisters much the same way the carnival idea came to me and my friends. After visiting a food festival and noticing a shaved ice vendor New Orleans Style Shaved Ice, Mikayla was inspired to start a similar business. After asking Mom to help, they've been pushing along for more than two years now.

The girls have learned that everything isn't very easy. For example, Mikayla had to re-design her snow cone cart several times. Shantae says "She also learned how to give great customer service and encourage people to buy. Kennedy has learned that she can't continue to eat all of the profits, and, also, that she can't use money the business has made to purchase her own snow cones!"

You can imagine how successful selling cool, refreshing, snow cones in the hot Arizona climate can be. Mix in this the novelty of two elementary school children operating the business, and you have a great head start into the business world. Very rapidly, they found their mother's friends inviting them to set up their cart at area events. As word spread, local media picked up the story. Mikayla and Kennedy soon appeared on *Sonoran Living* (which airs on the ABC affiliate). This led to both increased confidence and visibility.

Shantae adds the girls learned much from organizations designed to help child entrepreneurs. "The Arizona Children's Business Fair taught them about profit, cost, and how to pitch," she says. "It also showed them why it's important to keep selling – even on slow days – to just keep going, and keep looking for new opportunities."

HorseCrazyGirls.com

"Teenpreneur" Sydney Englund started her business at the age of nine and has been operating it for nearly a decade. HorseCrazyGirls.com is a website where "horse-crazy" girls can share their love of horses. They can share their favorite books, movies, their artwork, stories, and find plenty of horse games. It receives over 26,000 visitors a month from around the world."

"Being a young horse-obsessed girl, I wanted a place where I could not only share my love of horses, but also nurture it," says Sydney. "There was no website that offered everything I was looking for so I started my own."

She remembers "being super excited when I started my business. I wanted to put everything and anything on my site. That was not the best plan and ran into problems, including getting penalized by Google. I have had to do a lot of work to get the website performing well again. There have been a lot of ups and downs. I've tried things that worked surprisingly well and some that didn't, but everything I've done has taught me something about being an entrepreneur."

Sydney's business is going so strong she is getting ready to launch her own products. "I believe my passion for horses and great resources for horsecrazy girls is what has made my business successful," she says.

KidNewsMaker

Alejandra Stack is the CEO/Founder/Reporter of KidNewsMaker, based in the greater Atlanta, Georgia area, specifically, Carrollton, Georgia. Alejandra began her first newspaper column (in the *Florida Star* and *Georgia Star*) when she was eight years old. "I get my nose for news from my mom and she took me in the newsroom for the first time when I was three weeks old," says Alejandra. "She's a single mom so when she didn't have a sitter, she'd bring me along and I got to meet lots of people like celebrities, politicians, and other important people. They'd talk to me and I'd talk back. People called me "Allie in Action" and told my mom I was a natural. One night she was working late for the elections and told me to go read something so she could work. I noticed the only stories in their papers were of kids who were doing crimes or doing sports. So I told her they need to show positive stuff on kids if they want kids to read the paper. She told me to go write a story and I wrote three."

By age 9 or 10, "Allie in Action" started making videos. She also had completed a kidprenuer business course and met tons of great kids and felt they should be highlighted. She used money she had made working on a film to start KidNewsMaker when she was 11. She has since won three journalism awards.

"My company is a kid-centric multi-media platform," says Alejandra. "KidNewsMaker consists of online, print, and video interviews with kids making major moves across various platforms. My motto is 'We're not waiting, we're creating.' I don't want to just show celebrities because not everyone can be that. I want kids to be inspired by seeing people in their community or school (or whatever) accomplish attainable goals."

When she started her company, Alejandra took advantage of a local program for kids. It taught her a lot about marketing. "I was known as 'Allie in Action' and so I had to learn about rebranding and creating a campaign that was attractive to viewers," she says. "Through the ExCel Youth Mentorship Program, I learned many aspects of starting a business and being consistent. The course was taught by my mentor, Gabrielle Jordan, a teen who travels the world and gives motivational speeches. My mom joined a Momager Academy to learn how to balance this stuff for me."

Social media has made KidNewsMaker successful, along with her going from backstage baby to being the one asking the questions. Alejandra has gotten endorsements from local government leaders, youth and church organizations, and now is going international including kids from the United Kingdom and Caribbean.

Of course, it doesn't hurt that her mother is Arthia Nixon, an award-winning journalist, publicist, publisher, media personality, author, and communications coach/consultant. "First off, as a parent I am thrilled she has chosen to follow my path at such an early age," says Arthia. "The thing is, she is carving her own niche early on and giving people an insight into the future leaders of tomorrow. I'm a single mom and things are tough but through this, she has inspired me to even go back to school and do business courses to ensure that I am representing her properly as a mom and COO/Managing Editor. I used to see it as a hobby, but now she's got investors interested and this is a business. I'm thrilled."

Middle School Entrepreneurs

Used Golf Ball Sales

Not all business ideas need to be elaborate. Some can be very simple. In fact, simple business ideas are often the most successful. Why? Because they don't require a lot of effort to start and it's easy for customers to see the benefits. Mario Cruz, a marketing manager for a spill containment company in Jacksonville, Florida says his 12-year old son had one of those simple ideas when he "started selling golf balls at the 14th hole of the golf course we live on."

Proximity prompted this pre-teen to begin his business venture. "We live on a golf course but no one in our family plays golf," says Mario. "We collected the golf balls that landed in our pool and yard just for the fun of it to see how many we could get. One day, he emptied the vases that we had put them in, put them in his backpack and walked onto the course to 'set up shop'."

Golfers tend to share certain traits and they were impressed by this boy's ingenuity. "Presumably, the people that play golf are successful and have worked hard to get there," says Mario. "There are countless stories of people who are very impressed with my son and his business savvy. Some who aren't 'in the market' for golf balls will give him cash and/or buy him a drink or snack to show their appreciation for his efforts. One gentleman, after learning that my son will go into the ponds to fish balls out of the water gave him his ball retriever to make it easier."

Grom Social

Growing up on the Indian River Lagoon along Florida's Space Coast, it's easy to understand how Zach Marks and his family became surfing enthusiasts. Living in the shadows of the place that literally launched America's greatest achievement – the Apollo "Man on the Moon" project – it's also not surprising that Zach, Founder of Grom Social, would feel no task is too ambitious.

Ambition fuels curiosity. Curiosity, in turn, inspires you to explore. Sometimes exploration reveals great discoveries. Other times, exploration leads you into areas that can get you in trouble. If you're lucky, that trouble leads you to one of those great discoveries. Such is the story of the journey that inspired Zach to create Grom Social.

"I was 11-years-old and had a secret Facebook account with a few hundred friends," says Zach. "My dad (Darren) caught me and made me stop using Facebook as I was too young. I once again sneaked onto Facebook and was once again caught by my dad. This time, he jokingly told me to go start my own social media network if I wanted to use one so badly."

They say necessity is the mother of invention, and, if Zach wanted to enjoy the "Facebook experience," it would be necessary for him to invent a way to do so. Enter "Grom Social," and the rest, as they say, is history. "I have always been a computer enthusiast and learned a lot about coding," says Zach. "I brainstormed a lot of ideas with my siblings, my parents, and my friends. Soon enough, we were ready to launch the platform. We named it Grom Social because 'grom' is slang for a young surfer. Our whole family loves to surf."

There's nothing like the excitement of breathing life into a new business. Of course, if you think that's exciting, imagine what it's like to see that business begin to take off. "It was exhilarating," says Zach. "The idea clicked right away. Once we were ready to launch, we told our friends and their families. They then told their friends and family. We just saw the amount of people signing up to use Grom Social grow and grow and grow. The numbers ballooned even more after we received attention on *USA Today*. It was so unexpected, but it was also just a lot of fun. I woke up excited each day to check to see how many more people were using the site and what people were saying about Grom Social."

What does Zach say about Grom Social? "Grom Social is a social media network that's 'for kids by kids' used by children between the ages of 5-16," he says. "Grom Social is filled with wonderful interactive games and videos that are both fun and educational, and in particular emphasizes good digital citizenship. In addition, Grom Social is the safest social media network for children as it allows parents/guardians to monitor their kids' usage on the site."

Zach was 11-years-old when he started the business. Today he and his family live in San Juan Capistrano, California. He's moved to the next phase of his life, and so has Grom Social. "I'm 17 now and have just started my freshman year of college," says the young entrepreneur. "The business is still operating. In fact, we just became a publicly traded company. Today, Grom Social has about 12 million users and trades as GRMM on the OTCBB. The key to the success of the company was all of the hard work we put into it. My dad is a great influence on me. So are my siblings. We just constantly come up with new and more ideas to make the site grow. We make it fun for us. And what's fun for us is also fun for the other kids who use the site."

Frilliance

Like many her age, Fiona Frills of Saratoga, California, loves YouTube. In fact, she loves it so much she started her own YouTube channel when she was only 10 years old. She began posting a series she called "Gross Food." She developed quite a following.

In the meantime, she was fascinated with makeup. When she was 12 she decided to follow a path she had seen other YouTubers take. She noticed they promoted and sold products. Fiona thought this would be fun to try. She combined her two loves and – presto! – she created Frilliance, a brand of cosmetics and makeup tools for teens.

Fiona started the makeup brushes and tools line because she loves makeup and fashion. She posts videos about makeup. Almost half a million people subscribe to her YouTube channel. That gives her a large ready-made audience to pitch her products to.

Now 17, Fiona is still running the business today. She knows it takes a lot of patience to work through all the details of the business. She's discovered making everything come together for a business requires much more than she thought. She credits the success of Frilliance on her passion and love for makeup and beauty, so she feels like it isn't that much work.

AfterLite BodyCare

If anyone can create their own TV channel on YouTube, they can create their own store on Etsy. That's exactly what Destiny Helligar of Burbank, California did. Destiny, the CEO of AfterLite Bath and Bodycare Company, discovered the bodycare products she was using were very harsh on her skin. "I realized that I wasn't the only person with this problem, so I started to make natural soaps," says the pre-teen entrepreneur.

It wasn't easy to start. Destiny says, "I remember all the hard work you put into making the product and how many times you have to fail before you get a product right." Today, Destiny offers a full line of products through her all-natural bath body company. "We sell all-natural soaps, bath bombs, deodorant, and whipped oils," she says.

Destiny believes her company will remain vibrant because "we market to fix common skin problems."

Laine Avenue Backpacks

Emily Laine Miller of Columbus, Ohio was 13 years old and she had a problem. She actually had two problems. Like many entrepreneurs, she used one problem to solve the other. In doing so, she not only helped herself, she helped others who faced the same challenges she did.

"From an early age my parents have always taught me the importance of saving money for college," says Emily. "But as a busy teen, it was hard to find a part-time job that worked with my schedule. So, I came up with the idea to start a business that would help me earn money for college and also solve another problem my friends and I faced each year: finding a backpack that was stylish and functional, and that would stand up to the wear and tear from school and activities. I also thought it would be cool to find a way to change up the look of my backpack throughout the year."

Getting an idea for a product is only the first step. If you want that product to be successful, you need to talk to the people who you expect to buy the product before you start making it. That's what Emily did. In the process, she discovered she wasn't alone in her problems. Many of her friends had similar concerns. Her initial simple idea of a single physical product (the backpack) became a very broad solution for her intended market. It would also help her sell that product.

"Once I started talking to my friends about the idea, I realized so many teens like me also struggled to find a part-time job and save money for college," says Emily. "So, I had the idea to set up the company so other teens (in partnership with a parent) can sign up to be a Laine Avenue Backer and earn 25% commission on every backpack sold. It's really providing an alternative to the traditional part-time job and giving teens the opportunity to learn about entrepreneurship. Our online Life Skills Academy also teaches skills not always taught in high school, like financial management, personal development, and family and relationships. We really want to help teens and young adults learn all the skills needed to be successful in the future."

It took a few years to get all the kinks out, but Emily officially launched the business in the spring of 2017. Now sixteen, she says, "Laine Avenue Backpacks are the only backpacks on the market that can be customized through an interchangeable zipper flap, making it easy for teens to have a backpack to match every mood. The backpacks are made with durable brushed cotton and an ergonomic design that can carry up to three 3-inch binders, plus a laptop, folders and notebooks—holding everything needed for school. Laine Avenue convertible backpacks also include a detachable cross-body purse for carrying small essentials."

Knowing that she's helping herself and helping others obviously makes Emily feel good. There's nothing more satisfying than success. "One of the coolest parts about the business is seeing kids at my school who I don't even know wearing a Laine Avenue Backpack, or getting an order in from across the country," says Emily. "We only sell online and through our network of Backers, so word of mouth and social media has been key in getting the word out about my company. We've been lucky to get some great media attention. Seeing my backpacks featured on *The Today Show* was also a favorite moment."

Emily understands how much work it takes to launch a business. She appreciates all the help she's received, and is happy that she can return the favor to others. She says, "Operating a business is hard, but I'm lucky to have the support of my parents, family and friends. We're continuing to think about new products and designs to offer and other ways to get the word out about not only the backpacks, but the opportunity we are offering teens to earn money and gain life skills."

High School Entrepreneurs

Relaxing Meditations

Chris James, Co-founder of relaxingmeditations.com in Ames, Iowa, is just what you'd expect in a boy from America's heartland. He served as Senior Patrol Leader for his Boy Scout Troop. He has helped unload trucks for the local church's food shelf. And he loves his mother. More on that last thing in a moment.

Today he is a 19-year-old student at Iowa State University where he's working on a Bachelor's Degree in Entrepreneurship and Marketing. To give you a sense of his dynamic nature, he won first place in the ISU Spring Innovative Pitch Competition and received a $12,000 grant as part of the colleges "Cystarters Program" – a 10-week long business incubator for active entrepreneurs.

The story of Chris' entrepreneurial zeal begins in high school. He undertook several projects, in the creation of a comedy YouTube channel as well as various successful blogs. He also developed an app that was dubbed "Tinder for Kittens and Puppies." But it was his mother's work that inspired Chris to start his first business when he was 15 years old. "Two things prompted me to start," says Chris. "The first was I wanted to retire my mom. She works so hard for my family and I knew this would be a good way to make a passive income (though again, I had no idea what that meant at the time). The second was I thought it would be cool to make money online."

What was it exactly that Chris did while still in his early high school years? "My mom is a clinical hypnotist meaning she helps people lose weight, stop smoking and release a variety of limitations," recalls Chris. "She was currently only making money by having people come into her office and receive a CD version of the session. Although she made good money doing it, I knew if she converted those CD's to MP3's she could sell online to virtually anyone in the world and it would be scalable. (At the time I didn't know of the word 'scalable,' but the way I described it to her was if I placed her program online it would cost just as much, and take up just as much energy to sell to 1 person or to 1 million people. This just so happens to be the definition of 'scalable'). So, me, being the naïve teenager and knowing nothing about internet marketing, asked if I could sell her MP3's online."

Chris targeted really niche areas with smaller audiences, such as horseback riders who lost their confidence and it eventually turned into relaxingmeditations.com. "It went terrible at first," he says, "and I ended up burning up a lot of her cash, but I kept experimenting and eventually we started making a profit. I remember when I first started I'd spend $100 on ads, and only make a $10 sale. I had no clue what I was doing, but I kept learning."

Starting any business, but especially your first business, quickly dispels those naïve notions we all have. "I thought it would be super easy, but instead it was insanely difficult," says Chris. "I'd think, 'all right, all I have to do is place this online and it will sell itself.' Wrong. I thought I'd run some ads for the business and if only 5% converted, I make 200% profit. Only ½% converted and I lost money. It's just hurdle after hurdle. It really humbled me in that aspect."

Thanks to the support of his mother, Chris weathered those first inevitable hurdles. "What made it successful was that I kept going," he says. "My mom kept throwing cash at it. She knew I was getting a valuable education out of this experience. No matter what setbacks, I pushed through, tried something new, ran another experiment and raised my margins."

According to the website, Relaxing Meditations has helped more than 5,000 people. And at $149 a pop, simple math tells you Chris has helped his mom's business bring in more than three-quarters of a million dollars in revenue. Now that's what we call a good way to measure success!

Hygee Phone

Bennett Cohen, C.E.O & C.B.B (Chief Bacteria Buster) of Hygee, LLC, quickly assimilated into his new school after moving from Maryland to Malibu, California. He played varsity tennis, became part of the Mock Trial team, and joined the Model United Nations club, all the while earning a spot on the school's honor roll. Bennett's mom Jill says, "Like most teens, Bennett's phone is almost a 5th appendage! But when he found out how germ filled they are and how those germs can cause acne he set out to create a product that reduces that."

"I've always been a bit of a germaphobe, and research showed me that cell phones are the single grossest thing we use on a daily basis," says Bennett. "Studies show that phones are 10x-18x dirtier than public toilets and contain harmful bacteria such as E. coli, MRSA, and Staph. In short, phones can cause disease and gross acne (acne was a big part for me). Think about it, you bring your phone to work, on the metro, to the gym, but never really clean it. I knew alcohol kills germs, but turns out it is super bad for the phone, and can damage the electronics."

Shortly after turning 17, Bennett began working on a product to help alleviate this problem. "Hygee, LLC (hygeephone.com) is a tech-healthcare company that sells antibacterial phone cases and an antibacterial screen polish/cleaner," says Bennett. ("Hygee" is a play on the word "hygiene.")

Given that Bennett created a physical product (as opposed to an internet or media-based service), he discovered a different set of hurdles on the way to obtaining a patent. He says his most memorable experiences include "the months spent just prototyping the case and attempting to apply the natural mineral solution to the case permanently. That was one of the hardest things to accomplish regarding the product. I've also exhibited Hygee at startup conventions, which have helped me grow as a presenter and understand the world of business much better."

Bennett also learned the importance of working with well recognized institutions to gain both credibility and government approval. "We've partnered with leading green chemists to create coatings that have been scientifically supported by the University of Florida, the University of Leeds, and NASA," says the website he created for the product. In addition, Bennett has sought and obtained approval of his product from the U.S. Food and Drug Administration.

Like almost every entrepreneur, any short conversation about his business immediately reveals Bennett's passion. "The sheer penetration of the issue has made this something that everyone can relate to," he says. "Nearly everyone has a smartphone, and 92% of people use their phone in the bathroom. Ew! Hygee solves the serious issue of germs on phones for everyone, ranging from teens with acne to parents letting toddlers use their phones to the public transport commuter."

His mom sees it, too. "I am constantly amazed by Bennett's hard work and commitment to Hygee Phone," says Jill. "Now, if he would clean his room and make his bed every now and then instead of calling chemists all over the world and working on product design that would be great!"

Junior Achievement

High school students interested in creating a business but don't have a specific product or service in mind might want to explore school or community-based programs specifically geared for this purpose. For example, Tara Nolan, Marketing Manager of Junior Achievement of Northern New England in Waltham, Massachusetts, tells us her group offers its program to students aged 14-18 years old.

Tara and her colleague Phil Symons, (Program Manager at Junior Achievement of Northern New England), shared a recent experience they've had with teenagers who created their own company. "Vibes Inc. was founded in 2017 by a group of students from Boston and Greater Boston who came together through the JA Academy program," says Tara. "Their signature product, the Hearmuff, infused high powered headphone speakers with comfortable and warm behind-the-head earmuffs offering maximum comfort."

Tara explains how Vibes, Inc. came about. "These students participated in our organization's signature entrepreneurship program, the JA Academy Program," she says. "This 13-week program allows students to create, operate, and liquidate their own company. They create a product that satisfies a community need, then they market and sell this product to a target audience. They raise real capital to fund the venture, all while learning how to operate a business using our blended learning platform, where this program's online curriculum is housed."

The beauty of an established program like Junior Achievement is that teens can quickly realize what aspect of business and entrepreneurial activity most excites them. "Students' experiences varied in what they remember most, but all felt that this program significantly changed their lives," says Tara. "One exciting moment for everyone involved was when the group was invited to compete in the Junior Achievement National Leadership Summit – out of 100+ Junior Achievement chapters, Vibes Inc. was one of only 15 student companies chosen to participate in the competition."

While businesses created in these programs tend to be ad hoc and/or short-lived, that doesn't mean there's no measure of success. "The business is no longer in operation, but the success of the business was marked by their sales numbers as well as the group dynamic," says Tara. "Another success that Vibes Inc. saw was the second-place title at a Babson College business competition, beating out several other high school and college companies."

Child entrepreneurialism represents one of the most fulfilling ways to earn the income necessary to establish a Child IRA. For all these examples, though, the most likely path for most families is for the child to work for someone else. We explore this avenue in the next chapter.

CHAPTER 16.
FOR PARENTS AND GRANDPARENTS – THREE STEPS TO TURNING YOUR TEEN INTO A MILLIONAIRE

Before she became a teenager, Baylee Morrison had released her first single, starred in TV commercials, and made nearly two hundred appearances, including on a prime-time television episode and singing the National Anthem three times for the NFL's Buffalo Bills. In many ways, Baylee represents the path many parents help guide their young children towards. As often happens, the path begins with a genuine interest in entertaining, and not necessarily a way to earn income. Let's take a closer look at how this young actress/singer/dancer/model traveled along her path.

"Baylee was first interested in singing when she used to sing in the car on the way home from school in the back of her grandparents' car," says Bonnie Morrison, Baylee's mom. "Once, while on a family vacation, her grandpa took her down to the restaurant where they were having a karaoke night. Baylee sang a few songs and fell in love with the feeling of performing and making people smile when they listened to her sing. After attending several different child theater workshops when she was 7 years old, she had a few different vocal coaches. She has had her current vocal coach for the past 4 years. Baylee's first paying job was a commercial for Stickley Furniture when she was 7 years old."

Although singing might have been Baylee's entrée into the entertainment world, it led to modeling and acting. Those two activities, in turn, led to her first paycheck. To get there, her path took her, temporarily, to Los Angeles. "While in LA, she was a fit model for Forever 21 for three months," says Bonnie. "She has been in a few commercials and appeared on an episode of *The Bachelorette*. Baylee has received payment for the commercials she was in, the episode of *The Bachelorette* she was in, and when she modeled for Forever 21."

As with most other situations where a child gets paid, it's necessary to obtain and file the proper forms. "You have to have a child performing work permit to have your child work and earn money," says Bonnie. "Baylee had a child performer work permit while we were in LA and currently holds a child performer work permit in New York. You can download a form and mail in the necessary paperwork. You have to renew every year."

Baylee performs all the time, but usually only accepts donations toward her college fund. She deposits all these donations into a custodial account. Sometimes, she uses the funds to cover expenses and further her career. "Funds are put toward her future college plans, but some of the money is also used to work on her skills for her career (singing, dancing, acting, and modeling lessons)," says Bonnie.

When she was 12, Baylee released her debut single "Discommunication" on iTunes and Spotify. She soon found out this threw a bit of a monkey wrench into her plans. "We were trying to keep her as an amateur for singing so she could compete in events," says Bonnie. "She wasn't looking for paying gigs, she was just singing because she loves it!" Shortly after releasing the song, Baylee found out her path had changed. "When she went to compete at the New York State Fair, somebody told them she wasn't an amateur anymore," says Bonnie. "Now we will be looking for paying gigs! (in my spare time, which I have none of). I guess since she released a song on iTunes, she is no longer an amateur, even though she only makes pennies on the dollar! Baylee is hoping to start performing at birthday parties, charity events, sports events, and other events in the near future and receive payment for her performances."

Baylee Morrison began her journey when she was only seven years old. In six years, she's accomplished plenty, but there's more to go. At the time of this writing, she's getting ready to shoot a music video of "Discommunication." In addition, she has another original song ready for the recording studio. "It is a tough business for sure!" says Bonnie. "There is a huge learning curve! We'll be again traveling to LA for her to perform in front of agents and managers and hoping at some point she gets her break. She works hard and deserves a break!"

Bonnie Morrison has taken a very active role in the development of her daughter's childhood career. At the time she was interviewed for this book, setting up a Child IRA wasn't in the forefront of her mind.

*   *   *   *   *

Congratulations! If you're reading this chapter that means you're an upbeat parent or grandparent seeking to give your children or grandchildren the benefit of your life's experience. At one point or another, we've all lamented "if only I knew then what I know now." While you can't anticipate every possible situation that may relate to the lifetime of your child, you can address one of these many items right now: your child's retirement. What parent or grandparent wouldn't want to help their child or grandchild become a millionaire by the time that child retires? Establishing a Child IRA can accomplish this.

Here's how to do it.

These three easy-to-understand steps will help start you (and your child) on the way. While the previous chapter focused on kids who took the initiative to create their own businesses, this chapter is for proactive parents who want to help place their children in a position to establish a Child IRA. As you can tell from Bonnie Morrison's experience, it's possible to start a child on this journey early in life, but you need to be prepared for long hours and hard work. The impetus to encourage a child to start a Child IRA goes well beyond the prospects of retiring in comfort. "Much like anything a parent tries to teach a child along the lines of good habits, saving for the future is important," says Maura Cassidy. "Saving in a tax-advantaged account may make sense for you and your children."

Step #1: Assess Risks

Parents need to be aware of several considerations before agreeing to let their minor children earn an income. First and foremost, among them are the potential tax consequences. "Parents need to know the tax code states a child/dependent cannot provide more than 50% of their own support," says Suzanne Weathers. If the intention is to earn only enough income to contribute to the Child IRA, however, it's unlikely this 50% threshold will be met.

Beyond taxes, there are the usual concerns when it comes to activities outside of school. "Deciding to work before you are 18 is a huge time commitment that takes time away from your schoolwork," says Evelyn Cook. "The most important question to ask is whether that sacrifice is worth the additional income."

Speaking of school, as the child approaches college age, earned income may have a material impact on financial aid packages. Scott Vance says, "Probably a big thing to think about is college funding. The income of a child is included in the financial aid computations at a much higher rate than a parent's income. The data for computing financial aid has recently changed now so that when the child is a sophomore in high school, their tax situation is used to compute their freshman year of college financial aid eligibility."

The college equation continues beyond high school and into the child's college years. This potentially presents "a more complicated situation for parents of college age students who may receive partial scholarships, making this the perfect time for these parents and students to meet with a tax professional for a full review of how these changes may impact the bottom-line come tax time," says Weathers.

Step #2: Identify Opportunities

Once parents determine it makes sense for their children to begin earning the income necessary to contribute to a Child IRA, it's important to become familiar with Child Labor Laws. It is best to consult with a competent attorney that covers your local laws. Here are a few general points to ponder.

While it's easiest for the child if the parents own their own business (we'll discuss this special circumstance in the next chapter), this is not an essential condition. "Owning your own business is not necessary to set up an IRA for your child," says Jose Silva, Founder & CEO of Silva Fiduciary Advisors in Daytona Beach and Orlando, Florida. "As long as they have some kind of income – whether it be from yardwork, babysitting, walking the dog, or whatever – young people can start their own IRA and, if minors, their parents can set the IRA up as custodian or guardian for them."

Beyond these traditional jobs, and before you jump into positions that can generate substantial income, it's important to review important rules regarding the employment of minors. Ryan Neumeyer, says, "The federal child labor provisions, also known as the child labor laws, are authorized by the Fair Labor Standards Act (FLSA) of 1938. All states have child labor standards. When Federal and state standards are different, the rules that provide the most protection to young workers will apply. The FLSA, subject to a few exceptions, confines the employment of 14- and 15-year-olds to:

- Employment after school unless through school sponsored programs to three hours or less during a school day.
- Eight hours or less on non-school days.
- 18 hours a week or less during school weeks.
- 40 hours or less during non-school weeks."

Neumeyer adds, "At 16 years of age, youth may be employed for unlimited hours in any non-agricultural occupation other than one declared to be hazardous by the Secretary of Labor. Hazardous occupations are as follows:

- Manufacturing and storing of explosives.
- Motor-vehicle driving and outside helper on a motor vehicle.
- Coal mining.
- Occupations in forest fire fighting, forest fire prevention, timber tract operations, forestry service, logging, and sawmilling.
- Power-driven woodworking machines.
- Exposure to radioactive substances.
- Power-driven hoisting apparatus, including forklifts.
- Power-driven metal-forming, punching, and shearing machines.
- Mining, other than coal mining.
- Operating power-driven meat processing equipment, including meat slicers and other food slicers, in retail establishments (such as grocery stores, restaurants, kitchens, and delis) and wholesale establishments,

and most occupations in meat and poultry slaughtering, packing, processing, or rendering.

- Power-driven bakery machines including vertical dough or batter mixers.
- Power-driven balers, compactors, and paper processing machines.
- Manufacturing bricks, tile, and kindred products.
- Power-driven circular saws, bandsaws, chain saws, guillotine shears, wood chippers, and abrasive cutting discs.
- Wrecking, demolition, and shipbreaking operations.
- Roofing operations and all work on or about a roof.
- Excavation operations."

The good news, according to Neumeyer, is that certain businesses (family-owned) and industries (modeling, acting) are exempt from some of these guidelines. He lists these (and what guidelines are they not exempt from) as follows:

- There are various exemptions under the FLSA's prohibitions on labor for children in agriculture work on family-owned farms and with the consent of the parent for a child to work on farms.
- Children 16 and 17 years of age employed by their parents in occupations other than those declared hazardous by the Secretary of Labor are exempt under the FLSA.
- Children under 16 years of age employed by their parents in occupations other than manufacturing or mining, or occupations declared hazardous by the Secretary of Labor are exempt.
- The FLSA exempts performers and actors from the child labor rules.
- Newspaper delivery boys/girls are exempt.

Do some of these exemptions look familiar? Are you beginning to get a better idea of what's possible for your children? Still, there remains one overriding consideration all parents must be aware of before allowing their child to work for someone else. "The number one concern should be safety," says Neumeyer. "If an employer is willing to have a child work in a business, it should have policies and procedures to keep them safe. You should request a copy of all policies and procedures. Companies should, at a minimum, have an employee handbook which includes safety rules, or a separate safety manual. Determine if there will be adult supervision while the child is working or if the child will be left alone. Inspect the place of employment and interview the manager regarding what is expected and the job duties. Observe an employee actually performing the proposed job to determine if there are any safety risks. Contact OSHA and inquire whether there have been any violations by the employer. A parent can also search the local court docket and bureau of workers compensation to determine if there has been an inordinate amount of accidents. While there are no steps that will absolutely shield your child from every potential harm, by simply going through the aforementioned steps you can better protect your child in the work place."

Step 3: Start Saving in a Child IRA

Chapter 10 outlines various ways you can set up a Child IRA. You can do this at most major financial institutions. Just speak to your favorite bank, broker, or mutual fund. They should have ready-made instructions for you to establish a Child IRA (they often call it a "custodial" or "minor child" IRA). You can complete this part of the process as soon as your child earns that first paycheck.

Now, if your child is like any other child, the money earned will quickly be spent on items for immediate gratification or placed in a college savings fund. Neither of these are particularly bad options as the former helps teach the importance of financial management (i.e., budgeting) and the latter helps build responsible financial behavior through long-term goal setting. Still, neither one allows the child's earnings to be contributed to a Child IRA. That's where the parents (and grandparents) can lend a hand.

Remember, the rule for contributing to a Child IRA is that the income be earned. That income can be used for anything. It doesn't have to be saved for contributing to the Child IRA. The actual money used for the Child IRA contribution can come from somewhere else. Like the parents or grandparents. Yes, parents and grandparents can help establish Child IRAs "simply by funding the IRA or Roth IRA for the child who has earnings," says Timothy Shanahan, CEO, Compass Capital Corporation in Braintree, Massachusetts.

This can be as straightforward as giving it as part of a birthday present (talk about a gift that keeps on giving). "It's easy to do, but grandparents need to be certain their grandchildren have earned income to do this," says Jenkin.

It's important, though, for parents and grandparents to synchronize any gifting for the purposes of contributing to a Child IRA. Marianela Collado, says, "Similar to parents, grandparents can help fund the IRAs. They'll need to make sure they coordinate with the parents as to avoid over funding. The max is limited to their earned income or $6,000. We can't forget that."

Beyond gifts, grandparents can help by "communicating and encouraging their children to participate given the many benefits – educational and financial – for their grandkids," says Silva.

It may entail a unit of work for parents to help their kids find meaningful income opportunities. And, when it comes to dealing with teenagers, every once in a while, parents and grandparents just throw up their arms and in frustration and quote their favorite Groucho Marx line "What have future generations ever done for us?"

When that happens, sit down and take a breath. Especially if the parents have a family-owned business, for then the effort becomes much easier, as we will see in the next chapter.

CHAPTER 17.

A SPECIAL ADVANTAGE JUST FOR (SOME) FAMILY-OWNED BUSINESSES – THREE STEPS TO INCREASE CURRENT FAMILY WEALTH WHILE LOWERING TAXES AS YOU TURN YOUR TEEN INTO A MILLIONAIRE

F ollowing his graduation from Missouri State University, Gabe Lumby of Springfield, Missouri did what most folks who major in accounting and finance do. For nearly six years he worked in various positions for other accounting firms, methodically advancing in his career. Then it dawned on him. He had grown enough where it made sense for him to have his own firm. So, in July 2015, he hung his name on a shingle and began directly servicing the kinds of small businesses he had served for years. At the same time, a couple years later, he decided to help his younger brother Jacob by taking on an additional role as Chief Marketing Officer at Jacob's firm Cash Cow Couple. Jacob and Vanessa Gumby's website shares the lessons learned by the husband and wife team. The popular personal financial blog, while geared to young couples like Jacob and Vanessa, overlaps nicely with Gabe's niche – small business owners.

Gabe's accounting experience taught him several important lessons for running his business. Among the most important, however, was establishing IRAs as early as possible. This included not only his own retirement savings, but also a Child IRA for his son. "I didn't personally set up an IRA for myself (nor did my parents) before I was 18," says Lumby, "but I have done so for one of my kids and this is a tax strategy I recommend and help implement for clients."

Unlike other parents, families who own their own businesses have a distinct advantage when it comes to establishing Child IRAs for their children. There are many more options for those with family-owned businesses, allowing them to pay their children at much younger ages. "I thought of doing this for my child based upon my own research and understanding of taxes and financial planning. I worked at a very large CPA firm and then a small two partner firm before going out on my own and the 'kids on the payroll' was a popular tax strategy we used when appropriate. I guess I learned from – and was taught by – senior partners and I saw the benefit to the client and the client's child."

Starting his own firm provided Lumby with the opportunity to start a Child IRA for his oldest offspring. "My son was five years old when I set up the IRA for him," he says. "I've only used the strategy for one year when I used his images in some marketing materials. The total pay and amount deposited in the Roth was just $200. Again, I take seriously the idea that the pay to the child needs to be a fair arm's length transaction. I don't want to get audited and have to reverse everything and pay fines or penalties. My research indicated that somewhere around $200 would be fair for the modeling work he provided. I documented that research in my own tax file to save just in case. Obviously as he grows and is able to perform more work-related tasks, it will make sense to give him more responsibility and pay. But it would be very hard to justify that a 5-year-old provides ongoing services for our businesses. He does like to eat all the chocolate in the waiting area, but I don't think that would qualify."

While opportunities abound, risks exist, too. "Obviously, the biggest challenge (and potential audit issue) is getting the child earned income," says Lumby. "The tendency for business owners is to overpay their children for simple tasks. This is a mistake and a huge audit risk. You need to pay your child a legitimate wage for the work they do. For example, if you have professional photos taken of your child to use in marketing materials, you need to call around and see the going rate for what these child shoots would be. So, if a typical photo shoot for a child model would pay $300 in your area, it would be very unwise to pay your child $3,000 for this task. In summary, it is fine to pay your child for legitimate work to do, but you need to pay fair market wages for those tasks. I personally used my son in some marketing materials and paid him a few hundred bucks that we then put into a Roth IRA for him."

So, what does Gabe's son think about all this? "My son is just 5 years old, so he has no idea about the Roth IRA," says Lumby. "Because of his young age, I haven't really thought too much about discussing the Roth IRA with my son. I guess I just planned on telling him as I'm able to teach him about financial topics, but I'm sure that will be quite a few years down the road. I've thought about the fact that my son could turn out to be a real pain in the rear and I may not want to provide him these financial benefits, but I don't worry too much about it. If that is the case, I might kick myself in a decade. Ha ha."

*   *   *   *   *

In 2016, a study found 1.2 million husband and wife teams like Jacob and Vanessa Lumby running their own businesses.[1] This represents only a portion of family-owned businesses. According to data compiled on 2007 tax returns, in that year a total of 23.1 million people filed as sole proprietors, of which 16.9 million were profitable.[2] These numbers do not include farms, partnerships, and corporations. A 2003 study, based on estimates in previous research, assumed 60% of all partnerships and corporations can be defined as "family-owned," and calculated a total of 24.2 million family businesses in the United States.[3]

And yet, save for a very few forward-thinking parents and financial service providers like Gabe Lumby, you just don't see a prevalence of Child IRAs these numbers might suggest should exist. Most of the focus on Child IRAs, it seems, concentrates on teenage workers. This makes sense. For one thing, most children can't start earning income (a necessary prerequisite to contributing to a Child IRA) until they reach the age of 14. As a result, many financial firms see minors aged 14 and above as a much more lucrative market. (It turns out, this may offer an opportunity for savvy financial professionals.)

Parents (and sometimes even grandparents) who own their own businesses don't have to wait until their children turn 14 "because a business owner can place a child on the payroll to qualify for IRAs," says Timothy Shanahan. "My own children worked part time for my firm starting in elementary school. I used a number of techniques to optimize our tax/investment situation including Roth IRAs which were intended initially for college tuition but I was able to pay for college without touching them so now my children have accounts worth over $50k each."

With roughly 20 million family-owned businesses, there's a huge untapped opportunity for many children to begin their journey towards a multi-million-dollar retirement. This journey begins with these three steps:

Step #1: Does Your Business and Do Your Child's Earnings Qualify

Children generally cannot work until age 14. There's an important exemption that parents of family-owned businesses can take advantage of. If you own your own business, federal labor laws allow you to hire your own child – in most cases. You can't ask your children to work for you if it's a hazardous or dangerous job. You also can't require your children to work during hours they would normally be required to go to school. Additionally, state labor laws may be more restrictive than federal child labor laws, in which case the parent must abide by the higher standard.

Things can get dicey at the state level. Here's an example. In 1955, Frederick and Rosemary Nuzzo started a pizzeria in New Haven, Connecticut. When they retired they passed multiple locations to their sons. One of their sons, Michael, decided to prepare his young children (ages 13, 11, and 8) to eventually inherit the business. So he placed his oldest son in the kitchen, where he learned from his father how to make pizza. His younger son and daughter worked in the front helping their mother clear tables. When a patron complained about "child labor," Connecticut authorities came to the restaurant, found the children were working there, and cited Michael and his wife for child labor violations as Connecticut law prohibits children below the age of 14 from working. The parents sued (and garnered national press).[4] The suit was eventually settled with "everybody happy."[5] While it wasn't reported whether the children were allowed to continue working in the family business, three years later Nuzzo's pizzeria was named the "Best Thin Crust New Haven Style Pizza,"[6] and a picture from the same year under the heading "Best Pizza Place" in the annual "Best of New Haven" contest showed both Michael and his son.[7]

Needless to say, it's always best to consult a labor law attorney before hiring your children, no matter what their age.

Although most family-owned businesses are sole proprietorships based out of the home with no other employees, many are larger firms that employ non-family workers. This poses some important questions. Steven J. Weil, describes them as: "Can I remember to treat my child like any other employee and expect them to be productive, follow the rules, and be on time so that they learn good work skills? Am I paying my child an amount equal to what I would have to pay someone I was not related to for the same work?"

It goes without saying children must remain subject to existing employee rules and regulations. The subject of pay, however, presents a more contentious issue for parent businesses both with and without non-family workers. There are some aspects of non-family workers that do not apply to your children. "Many parents enjoy hiring their children to help in the family business," says Bonnie Lee, owner of Taxpertise in Sonoma, California. "It's good training for the day when they will take over. However, there are some who use this merely as a write-off and it's here that the IRS attempts to sniff out fraud. Well, maybe fraud is too strong a word because it's not like the miscreant will go to jail. But if you provide the kid a W2 so you can get the tax deduction and no services were provided by the child, the IRS will disallow the deduction. They want to see timesheets, paystubs, anything to prove the kid did the job. Absent those items, the deduction is taken away. But if an employer hires his child as a bona fide employee, he does not have to withhold and match Social Security, Medicare, or Federal Unemployment Tax (FUTA), that's only if it's your own child and the child is under age 18."

Saving money on payroll taxes is a good thing. The actual payroll number may present a challenge, particularly if the position is unique and there are no other comparable positions already on staff. In most cases, what you pay your child needs to pass the smell test. "Generally, income is considered in return for work," says Scott Vance. "For a child working in a family business, in my tax practice, I would expect a common-sense approach with some supporting documentation. For instance, I wouldn't expect a 12-year-old kid to provide legal services in a family law firm and billing at a rate of $200 an hour. I would look to see that the child's age, type of work performed, and amount paid to the child are comparable."

As a rule of thumb, you might want to start with the prevailing minimum wage, and work the hourly rate up as the required skills increase. Weil says, "The amount paid should not exceed what you would pay a non-related party to perform the same work. For example, putting merchandise back on shelves does not require any special skill. Thus, minimum wage might be right in that case. A teen with web design skills at $25.00 an hour could be a bargain."

Step #2: Choose a "Best-Fit" Job for Your Child

Once you decide your business can hire your child, you'll quickly find out how easy it is as a business owner to bring your child on board. Why is it so effortless? "It's easy because parents can dictate the job description for their child and the duties in order to be able to have earned income," says Jenkin.

This works both ways. "If the parents own their own business, it makes it easier for the child as they don't have to go out there and get a job," says Marianela Collado. Of course, older children might realize this advantage, but younger children might be missing out on good lessons if they think everything will be handed to them. But this is a problem with all endeavors that involve helping your children. At some point, they have to learn to help themselves. But that's the subject of another book, not this one.

Chapters 12 and 13 talked about jobs for teenagers. Those chapters discussed those jobs in a theoretical sense. This chapter presents some actual cases and the real jobs undertaken by children for their parents' businesses. Lumby works with small family-owned businesses who have hired their own children. Here are some examples of actual work he's helped business owners implement with their children:

- Advertising marketing materials for their business (mentioned above)
- Cleaning the business office space
- Doing general office duties (putting stamps on mail, checking the PO Box, filing duties, light computer admin work, etc...)
- Mowing the lawn at the commercial office

Lumby likes to advise his small business clients to establish Child IRAs for their child-employees. "Really, any job that you would pay someone else to do that the child can perform is an opportunity for earnings to then contribute to a Roth IRA," says Lumby. "The child will benefit from the time value of money/compounding interest. Plus, if the vehicle used is a Roth IRA, they will likely never pay tax on the initial deposit nor the earnings nor the distributions. It is like free money! There really isn't a better opportunity to set your child up for future success/retirement than getting started as soon as possible with a Roth IRA if they have legitimate earned income to use to contribute."

So, then, how exactly do parents go about hiring their children? We saw earlier in this chapter how Lumby did it for his own 5-year old son. In previous chapters we saw other case studies of parents who hired their children and the kinds of jobs they tasked their children to perform. Lumby tells us of two other circumstances for a couple of very typical family-owned businesses:

The Professional Service Firm Administrative Assistant:

Like Lumby himself, many parents' businesses are professional offices. Professional offices need – you guessed it – professional office workers. This includes a wide variety of jobs most children can perform. Lumby tells us of one of his clients who also provides professional services. "His 15-year old daughter provides administrative services to him for around 10 hours a week. She does anything and everything that a typical administrative professional would do including returning phone calls, maintaining a filing system, setting appointments, checking email, etc. He pays her $10/hr which is a competitive wage for our area. He should have no issues as everything has been well documented. This amount of work and pay allows her to completely fill up her Roth IRA each year."

The Rental Property Landscaper:

As we saw earlier with Rodney Davis, it's not unusual for parents to own rental property. While not their main job, they often create side businesses to manage and operate the property. You don't have to be an expert handyman like Rodney in order to employ your children. There are much more manageable (and traditional) home-related jobs kids can do. Lumby says, "We have a client who has a few teenage boys and owns a bunch of single family rental properties. Instead of paying a lawn care company, they pay their sons to do the mowing each week (they don't like trusting the tenant to maintain the property). He called up a few local lawn care companies to get competitive bids for all the properties. He pays his sons the average of the two bids received. This work doesn't provide enough income for each son to max out the Roth for each of them, but it does provide a few thousand dollars each year for each of them to contribute to their Roth IRAs."

Step #3: Open That Child IRA and Start Your Child on the Road to Becoming a Multi-Millionaire in Retirement

We won't repeat here what we've said several times earlier about the mechanics of creating and contributing to a Child IRA. Rather, we'll focus on a couple of different twists that pertain to parents and grandparents who own businesses.

If You Like the Child IRA, Just Imagine the Power of the Child 401(k)

Sure, parents can set up Child IRAs for their children-employees. But those aren't the only retirement plans available to business owners. Small business owners regularly use retirement savings vehicles for themselves, and there's no reason why they can't use them for their children, too (just like they would use them for any other employee). Two of the more popular plans are the SEP-IRA and the more familiar 401(k). Each allows for a higher potential contribution (based on the employee's annual earnings), but, more importantly, each permits an employer contribution. It's outside the limited scope of this book (remember, we're talking about "Child IRAs" here, not "Child SEP-IRAs" or "Child-401(k)s"), so you'll need to talk to your tax consultant to explore the ramifications of these vehicles. If you want to tease yourself on the possibilities, check out Bonus Chapter 19 (print version only) – A Turbo-Charged Child IRA – The

Child Solo 401(k). This might just blow your mind, especially if your child hits a gold mine like some of the case studies we examined in earlier chapters.

A Special Situation: The Grandparent Owned Business

For the most part, this chapter speaks only of the child labor exemption allowed for parents hiring their minor children. It's not evident how this applies to grandparents, although a case can clearly be made that the exemption is more likely to apply if the grandparents have legal custody of the children. While each situation has its own set of different circumstances, for our case let's assume the grandparents aren't allowed the child labor exemption. First, grandparents always have the option of gifting an amount equal to earned income that will be contributed to the Child IRA (although this still requires the child to earn that income from some outside source). Second, in the special case of a grandparent-owned business, it's possible there may be creative ways to stay within the letter of child labor laws and still have the grandparent's business pay for the grandchild to work. As in all cases, it's important to check with tax and legal advisors to ensure compliance.

In the end, it makes sense for parents who own businesses to hire their children. Weil says, "Paying your child does two things: 1) it gets money out of your tax bracket and into theirs (with the new tax law, the first $12,000 they earn is tax free at the federal level), and 2) it teaches them important life skills and about money and its value."

If this makes so much sense, why aren't more family-owned businesses using this tax saving technique that also allows their children to save for retirement through a Child IRA? Perhaps it's because they simply don't know. How would they discover this advantageous financial tactic? Obviously, they could read this book. More likely, though, they'd go to the people who answer most of their tax and financial questions.

* * * * *

So there you have it. A nice little handbook for the parents who want to turn their teenagers into millionaires before they graduate college. You do want to turn your teenager into a millionaire, don't you? Visit ChildIRA.com to discover more helpful tools, insights, and examples on this subject.

SECTION FIVE:

– BONUS CHAPTERS –

BONUS MATERIALS FOR THOSE WHO DESIRE TO GAIN A BIT OF AN EDGE

(BONUS) CHAPTER 18.
THE COMPELLING (AND AMAZINGLY EASY) SOLUTION TO THE INEVITABLE COLLAPSE OF SOCIAL SECURITY

This may sound like an April Fools' joke, but, trust me, it's not. That's just how unbelievable it is. It's the kind of Eureka! discovery that can only occur in the wee small hours of the morning after endlessly toiling away at numbers and statistics and statistics and numbers.

And the beauty of it is that it works!

What if I told you there was a low cost way to wipe out the need for Social Security within one generation — and not only would it not cost the government a dime but it would generate massively more tax revenue. Would you believe me? Or would you call me an April Fool?

Most folks would bet on the latter — and most folks would be wrong!

It's so simple and obvious, it's amazing no one has ever thought of it before. Heck, it's such a great idea, I'm even willing to concede the debate on whether there's really a retirement "crisis." Here's how the idea first struck me...

It was while writing an article that is the basis for *Hey! What's My Number? – How to Improve the Odds You Will Retire in Comfort* that the idea of The Child IRA hit me like a ton of bricks.

There I was, playing with numbers in my spreadsheet models when, like a chemist whose accidental spill leads to the discovery of a fabulous cure, I inadvertently started at year 0 instead of year 15. (You'll have to read *Hey! What's My Number?* to understand the significance of starting at year 15.) Curiosity getting the better of me, rather than correcting the error, I extrapolated upon it.

Lo! And Behold! came the answer that is guaranteed to solve our nation's alleged retirement crisis. OK, OK, I said I was willing to concede the point that there really is a retirement crisis. And, admittedly so, if you consider Social Security a component of retirement, then, sooner or later, like any other Ponzi Scheme, we will find ourselves in a crisis. Only, the thing is, this idea allows Social Security to die a natural death, wiping away forever our mournful addiction to this gangster era racket.

Ready?

Here's the idea.

I'll call it "The Child IRA." It's actually something a few elite folks have taken advantage of now, assuming their children have been modeling since before they could crawl. Its effect — without the tax-deferred benefits — can also be duplicated today, mainly via trust funds, but also through regular investment accounts.

But what I'm proposing is not at all like these. It's a tax-deferred account that doesn't require earned income on the part of the primary beneficiary (i.e., the "Child" of The Child IRA). It would allow any adult (parents, grandparents or any other random unrelated adult for that matter) to contribute an aggregate total of $1,000 (pre-tax) to any child every year until they reach the age of 19. Think of it as a combination of the power of compounding found in the 401(k) plan with the contribution flexibility of a 529 plan.

Here's how it works. Every child born in the U. S. of A. would be allowed to accept up to $1,000 per year until their nineteenth birthday into their own "Child IRA." Any adult can make a tax-deductible contribution into anyone's Child IRA, so long as the total contributions to any single Child IRA do not exceed $1,000 in any one year. The contributing adult does not have to be related to the child that owns the Child IRA.

Now, are you listening? Here's the beauty of the plan. All Child-IRAs would be required to be invested in long-term equities (preferably not through any government fund but through existing private investment vehicles like mutual funds or individual stocks). There'll be none of this "risk aversion" stuff because you can't withdraw from a Child IRA until age 70 (the "real" retirement age by the time today's kids get there). With this kind of requirement, we'd expect these Child-IRAs to grow at the rate of return of stocks. Historically, that's a tad above 11%, but let's be conservative and say it's 8%. Do you know what that means?

That means, by contributing $1,000 a year from the year of birth until the 19th birthday (a total of $19,000 in contributions), a Child-IRA will be worth in excess of $2.2 million when the owner retires at age seventy. That's on top of any other retirement savings that person might have. And with that $2.2 million head start, where is the need for Social Security?

And what a head start it is!

The Child IRA. It's the answer to all our retirement woes. It obviates the need for Social Security (at least that part that deals with retirement). It doesn't cost the government anything to implement. Best yet, it'll leave the government with an ongoing tax windfall.

Here's how:

According to the US Census, there are roughly 75 million children in the United States. If all Child IRAs are fully funded each year, that would defer taxable income by $75 billion. Another way of saying, based on the Tax Policy Center's average Federal Tax Rate of 20.[1] For 2013, (based on the data available at the time of this writing) this would equate to a short-term loss of $15 billion in revenues per year. By eerie coincidence, according to the President's 2014 budget, it costs $12.5 billion dollars to operate Social Security.[2]

But let's not get ahead of ourselves. I said this wouldn't cost anything and here's why. Looking at the costs in another way, a fully funded Child IRA ($1,000 per year until that child's nineteenth birthday) would require a total of $19,000 in total tax-deductible contributions. Again, assuming the average 20.1% tax rate, this reduces tax revenues by $201 per year for a total reduction of $3,819 over the nineteen years contributions are allowed.

By age 70, when the child retires, assuming an average annual return of 8% (versus the historic average annual return for equities of 11.17%), The Child IRA would be worth $2,267,361. Furthermore, if the retiree now takes out 4% a year ($88,506) and pays the current average tax of 20.1%, the government will earn $17,790 in tax revenues a year. That's nearly a 9,000% return on that $201 annual "investment" the government makes during the contribution period of the Child IRA. Not bad for doing nothing.

Finally, that $88,506 is 58% more than the current median income of $55,775. Traditional retirement savings vehicles will still be needed because, like Social Security, the Child IRA is not intended to fully fund retirement.

But, unlike Social Security, the Child IRA isn't a Ponzi Scheme, doesn't cost the government money (moreover, by eliminating the annual operating cost of Social Security, it'll save the government money), and, in fact, it will increase government revenues.

Like I said, it's so obviously simple, why hasn't anyone ever come up with it before? Moreover, why hasn't it already been done? I mean, we've got the 529 plan. To get to The Child IRA, all we'd have to do is say 529 plans can be used for both education (which they're currently limited to) and retirement. So again, why hasn't this been done already?

We'll save this answer for the public policy wonk. For now, let's not talk about what might be done if we waited long enough for the politicians to act. Let's focus on what you could do now, by yourself, without the need for legislation, regulatory approval, or any other third-party action. Dive into The Child IRA as it is today. And, believe me, you're going to want to do this because it really is as easy to do as what I just described – and just as lucrative for your children (and grandchildren).

(BONUS) CHAPTER 19.

WHAT TO DO IF YOU MISSED THE CHILD IRA TRAIN? IT'S NOT TOO LATE TO GIVE A COLLEGE GRADUATION GIFT WORTH $3 MILLION

June is the season of graduation parties. Whether newly minted from high school or college, these young minds leave the classroom full of vigor, ambition, and missing the one thing that's most important to them. Yes, we teach them to look to the next level quite well. We sate them with so much self-esteem they come brimming with confidence and high expectations. They're ready and willing to tackle new jobs, higher education, and a world they've been told is waiting for them with open arms.

Alas, amidst this unbridled enthusiasm sits an easily attainable goal all alone in a dimly lit corner. Aside from cobwebs and dust, its only covering is a faded sticky note with the words "open later – we have time" scrawled in child-like cursive on it. This is the goal we like to call "comfortable retirement."

We humans are a resilient species. We can accomplish almost anything given enough time, resources, and hard work. Unfortunately, we are also a species that enjoys to eat, to drink, and to be merry. We often put off to tomorrow things that we can (and should) do today. We quickly learn to prioritize goals not by some overarching strategy, but by the tick-tock of impending deadlines.

Of all the gifts we can offer graduates, even we miss the opportunity to help them focus on that which endures for a lifetime. We give cars (sometime, although rarely, a Shelby GT350® capable of going from zero-to-60 in 4.3 seconds behind the 526 horsepower 5.2L Ti-VCT V-8 engine), but, thanks to Henry Ford's brilliant innovation (not the automobile itself, but the concept of planned obsolescence), they last but a handful of years. We can give a wad of cash, but chances are that will end up merely buying the aforementioned car, and we end up with the same rusting result. We can give a good and meaningful book, but unless it can be read on the tiny screen, its greatest purpose will be to serve as a foundation to prop up some cheap furniture.

Enterprising parents and family members are now beginning to feel the best gift is to help reduce the graduate's loan burden. While that may be both helpful and practical, there is a greater gift, one more practical, one immensely helpful. This is the gift of The Child IRA, (although, at this point the "child" refers to the relationship and not the age, since college graduates tend to be adults).

Technically, you can't "give" an IRA. You can, however, give the cash necessary to start an IRA. Actually, the better way to do it is to bring the paperwork to the graduate so that you can be there when it's signed, then take it back and deposit your cash gift right into the new IRA account. By the time one graduates, one usually has (or will soon have) enough earned income to cover the maximum allowable annual IRA contribution (currently $6,000).

Let's say you're reading this book and you have come to the realization that you may have missed the train on this whole "Child IRA" thing. It's not too late to catch up. It's a bit more onerous but not terribly difficult. The numbers are easy to determine.

I can ask you to go back to Chapter 5 and take another look at the penultimate paragraph, but you'll end up thumbing through the pages of this book and then lose your place. Besides, what precisely is "the penultimate paragraph" anyway?

Instead, I'll do you a favor and tell you the key takeaway from that paragraph (whichever one it is) right here on this page. Or maybe the next page. One never knows exactly on which pages the words of a manuscript will fall once it's gone through the printing process.

For those parents whose children are beyond high school, it is possible to make amends for not reading this book a decade or so before it was written. No, you don't need a time machine to accomplish this, you just need the proper instructions. Fortune is with you today as I'm going to give those instructions to you right now.

(Author's Note: I know, I know, not every child is on the same "age" calendar when it comes to graduating from college. Some try to save money and graduate a year early while others may take some time off and graduate a year later. All that changes is step 5) of the instructions.)

1) Remember that graduation gift of an IRA you decided to give? Well, you need to offer to give this gift not just for graduation, but the several years after graduation.

2) Your (now adult) child will need to earn at least $6,000 during the year of graduation. For the purposes of this set of instructions, we'll assume your child graduates at age 18, 21, 22, or 23.

3) You bring your child the IRA paperwork, show them how to fill it out and where to sign. You may need to do this in the presence of the financial institution you will use to open the account. N.B.: Unlike the Custodial IRA that you must use for a minor child, this is a regular IRA since your child is now an adult.

4) You write a check for $6,000 and deposit it into the child's account.

5a) **When a child graduates from high school (age 18):** Continue to gift your child $6,000 every year until your child's 27th birthday.

5b) **When a child graduates from college a year early (age 21):** Continue to gift your child $6,000 every year until your child's 33rd birthday.

5c) **When a child graduates from college (age 22):** Continue to gift your child $6,000 every year until your child's 37th birthday. That year you only need to gift $2,000 for depositing in the IRA.

5d) **When a child graduates from college a year later (age 23):** Continue to gift your child $6,000 every year until your child's 40th birthday.

6) Do nothing and earn an average of 8% a year (remember, that's 3% below the average annual return for US equities).

7) When the child retires at age 70, that IRA will have grown to $2.25 million!

You might notice you don't have to give as much if you start earlier. In fact, when a child graduates college at the usual age (22), parents will need to gift a total of $92,000 over 16 years to catch up to the original Child IRA. If a child graduates a year early, those gifts total only $78,000 over 13 years to catch up to the original Child IRA. When a child graduates a year later, to catch up to the original Child IRA parents must gift a total of $108,000 over an 18-year period. (Well, heck, you can't take it with you so what better way to spend it!)

Of course, if the Child IRA starts immediately upon high school graduation, the gift total is only $60,000 spread out over 10 year. Hmm, what's the annual cost of college tuition these days? Kinda makes you think, doesn't it?

If you're like many people, you're looking at these total numbers and thinking, "That's more than I earn!" Well, rest easy. The beauty of the gifting concept is that it doesn't have to come from one source. The parents don't have to foot the whole bill (or even any of it). The grandparents, aunts, uncles, and perhaps a friendly neighbor or two – anybody – can provide the money that will be contributed into the IRA. There are no tax implications for these gifts because the IRS allows you to give up to $15,000 per year to individuals (as of 2019), and the maximum contribution of $6,000 is well below that.

Offering an ongoing graduation gift of a Child IRA helps the graduate develop a habit for retirement savings. When that graduate retires at age 70, those little annual IRA contributions will have grown to more than $2.25 million dollars (that's assuming an annual return of 8%). Not too bad and way better than some car (even a Shelby GT350®).

Now, if you are in a position to hire an outside contractor, whether in your own business or as an employee of a business, there's something else you can do. Something more powerful than a mere Child IRA. In fact, think of it as a Child IRA on steroids. Of course, since we're talking only of IRAs, it's really not the focus of this book. Still, I'm not good at keeping secrets, so you can take a peek at the next Bonus Chapter (print edition only) to discover what this is.

But you didn't hear it from me.

Are you ready to start a Child IRA?

(Bonus) Chapter 20.
A Super Turbo-Charged Child IRA – The Child Solo 401(k) (This Works for Adults, too!)

The problem with the Child IRA is you have to start it when the baby is newly born (or reasonably thereafter). Are you reading this and thinking, "My children are teenagers, there's no way they can catch up this late in the game"? That's not entirely true. Have you ever heard of the "gig" economy? It just may contain the answer.

Remember when you used to hire your kid to do a particularly dirty job you didn't want to do? Let's say an overnight windstorm blew over the trash cans. It's 8 o'clock in the morning. The waste disposal folks come in thirty minutes. You're in your PJs and quite comfortable. You turn to your oldest child and say, "Can you go outside and clean up the garbage? I'll give you five dollars."

Boom! You kid just became a gig worker!

These freelance ventures don't need to be one-and-done. You can hire your child to walk the dog. That's about $10 a week worth of work. It's a regular gig. Now we can get on to more serious things.

Let's switch things around for the moment. Instead of lazing around at home in your pajamas, you're busying yourself at work (pajamas optional, but only on pajama Friday). You've got a few odd jobs that need jobbing. You can hire your kids to do that. They can use that money to fund an IRA. But they'll have to come into the office every day, you'll eat dinner with them every night, and you'll have to bring them along on family vacation. In other words, you'll never get a break from them. And the most they can contribute for retirement is $6,000 a year.

But, what if there was a way to both see your kids less and maybe have them save more for retirement. Rather than bring them on as employees for ongoing tasks, hire them as contractors for short-term projects. Think of the assignments you need done that you might search the internet to find one of those "one-and-done" gig workers. Only don't scan the world wide web. Scan the kitchen table.

There are quite a few brand-building projects most businesses can readily use. We'll review one of them, one that I happen to have recent (and not so recent) experience with: video production.

Thanks to the advent of super-smart phones with extremely user friendly and intuitive software, many of today's teenagers have no problem creating internet-ready videos. Indeed, with the trend towards visual rather than written content, forward thinking business leaders want and need more video content to attract the younger generations (i.e., the markets that are growing).

You can hire a local company or a major media company to make these videos. It'll cost you anywhere from $500 to $10,000. The cost depends on number of cameras used, number of shooting locations, post-production complexity and total time of the video. To give you a sense of how this might vary, I share with you the costs of some video's I had done.

In the summer of 2017, I filmed an interview with Ted Benna. It was a two-camera straight shoot (meaning nothing was edited out). Post production included cutting back and forth between the two cameras, overlaying the audio (which was on a separate track) and adding an intro and an outro. The total cost was roughly $2,500 for a 30-minute video.

Contrast this cost to what I paid to have a couple of promotional videos done for a book I wrote in 2012. A 60-second book trailer included 4 location shots, one camera, and a separate audio. A 4-minute "sneak preview" video featured a two camera in studio set-up with a separate audio. In the post-production, some animation and several cuts were added. The total cost was roughly $5,000.

Lastly, I once created a Kickstarter campaign that needed a video. I priced out a 90 second animated video and got quotes from $500 to

$2,500. I opted to buy the software myself (for $300) and produce the video myself.

Here's the deal. My kids have been able to produce videos like these since high school. I could have hired them on and paid them to produce not one, but several videos. Increasing video content makes whatever you're doing more engaging to your audience.

Imagine your child making twelve one-minute videos a year for your business – one for each month. You'd pay $1,000 for each video, meaning your child would earn $12,000. That's twice the allowable deduction in a standard IRA.

There's another vehicle that's perfect for people with extra income when they don't need that extra income to support their current expenses. Think children who are students or adult children with second jobs (i.e., a job working for their parents). It's the Solo 401(k) plan. "We often see it in a moonlighting situation," says Bruce Gendein. "The extra income from the sole proprietor activities is not needed for life style and the Solo 401(k) deferrals allows them to save a large part of the business earnings."

Let's return to our not-so-imaginary situation where your child makes videos on the side. What if your child, as a sole proprietor, established a Solo 401(k)? Then that entire $12,000 could be saved for retirement. "The Solo 401(k) allows you to defer up to 100% of your income (up to $18,500)," says Patrick Dinan, president of Impact Fiduciary in Los Angeles, California.

The Solo 401(k) also allows for a Roth option, too. There are, however, a couple of major differences with Solo 401(k) plans. First, they're only available to businesses where the owner is the sole employee. This makes them perfect for the gig worker. On the downside, there may be more paperwork once the assets in the Solo 401(k) reaches a certain threshold.

Your child may be too old to fully benefit from a Child IRA, but if you own your own business, there's no reason why your child can't turbo-charge retirement savings by starting a "Child" Solo 401(k).

But, please, before you do anything, always check with your tax advisor.

SECTION SIX:

– APPENDICES –

HELPFUL TOOLS AND REFERENCES

APPENDIX I.
THE CHILD IRA – FAQ

The idea behind Child IRA as discussed within the context of this book first appeared in the article "What Every 401(k) Plan Sponsor and Fiduciary Should Disclose to Employees: How to Retire a Millionaire (Hint: It's Easier Than You Think)," (*FiduciaryNews.com*, February 25, 2014). A spreadsheet accident led to a follow-up article, the first to mention the phrase "The Child IRA." The almost penicillin-like serendipity led to the publication of the article "This idea will solve the retirement crisis, guaranteed!?" (*BenefitsPro*, February 26, 2014). It quickly became apparent The Child IRA could easily obviate the need for Social Security. This led to the article "It's time we create a Child IRA," (*Benefit Selling*, April 2014). Finally, the entire notion of The Child IRA was fleshed out and repurposed to become Appendix V in the book *Hey! What's My Number? – How to Improve The Odds You Will Retire in Comfort*, (Christopher Carosa, 2014, Pandamensional Solutions).

Since then, and especially given the publicity with the launch of *From Cradle to Retirement's* Kickstarter campaign, we've seen plenty of excellent questions about how The Child IRA works. We've distilled the most popular questions here.

Question #1: I like it! The Child IRA is a tremendous way for me to introduce a valuable tool to my clients. I do wonder, however, if it's a good idea to "guarantee" a person's retirement. In some ways worrying about our futures make us better as it's an incentive to become more engaged in our careers and engagement is healthy. How would the Child IRA impact a person's ambition?

Answer #1: First, like any other IRA, there are no "guarantees" regarding what the future might look like, there are only probabilities. The calculations assume an average growth rate of 8% – which is 3% below the historical average growth of 11% a year (that's enough to account for inflation, fees, and whatever else you want to account for). Then there's this mathematical reality: The $2.5 million 70 years from now merely replaces Social Security – the child will still need to save for retirement as an adult in order to secure a comfortable retirement. If that doesn't answer the "ambition" question, consider this. There's this behavioral trick bartenders do to encourage tips: They always place a few dollars in the "Tip Jar" before the customers arrive. Seeing money already in there encourages patrons to add to the kitty. Think of this Child IRA as the "Tip Jar." Once the child sees the money accumulating year after year, it is likely to trigger a behavioral response consistent with bar patrons: They'll be more likely to save even more!

Question #2: I also wonder if people would be more apt to tap into funds that they didn't save themselves?

Answer #2: Oddly enough, the *From Cradle to Retirement* contains interviews with quite a few "children" who are now adults and whose parents established IRAs for them. Most of them seem to value the "lesson learned" and are even interested in starting Child IRAs for their children. One person, who had a Roth instead of a traditional IRA, did use some of the money to pay for graduate school. This is the issue with using Roths, but not with using traditional IRAs, since the Roths allow for non-penalty withdrawals for education. In both cases, withdrawals normally aren't allowed until age 59½.

Question #3: If parents learn that their children did use the money for frivolous purchases, how would they react and what impact would this have on the relationship they have with their children (i.e., "I can't believe little Billy spent his retirement on a Corvette, what a jerk!")?

Answer #3: As mentioned, money from IRAs cannot be withdrawn without penalty until age 59½ (except in the case of the Roth and that's for the sole purpose of funding education expenses). That doesn't mean you can't take the money out before hand; it just means there's a significant disincentive for premature withdrawals. Still, that's better than no disincentives, which often occurs with Custodian Trusts established for children. For the most part, these trusts are released "no strings attached" once the beneficiary reaches early adulthood. There is an alternative which still uses the IRA vehicle. This involves either parent establishing an IRA (most likely a Roth) in their name and listing the child as a beneficiary. This way, the only way the child gets the money is if the parent dies. At least then the parent won't have to suffer to see how the money is squandered. ☺

Question #4: I watched the video on the Child IRA. It's a great concept, but a child can't open an IRA unless they have earned income. The video talks about putting money into a Child IRA at birth through age 19, but the child normally can't work until age 16 and receive a W2 in order to contribute to an IRA or a Roth IRA. Can you give me a little more detail on how that concept is to work based on that fact?

Answer #4: This is a great question as well as a common misperception. It's perhaps the single greatest reason why we haven't seen many people taking advantage of the Child IRA for their young children. In fact, children below the age of 16 do work and earn income. Yes, babysitting and mowing the neighbor's lawn counts as earned income, but children have real jobs, too. You don't think all those child actors work for free, do you? In addition to certain industries that regularly employ children under the age of 16, family-owned business generally have no age restrictions when it comes to employing their own children. *From Cradle to Retirement – The Child IRA – How to start a newborn on the road to comfortable retirement while still in a cozy cradle* explains how to establish a Child IRA today in precise, easy-to-understand (and duplicate), detail through actual real-life case studies, interviews with industry professionals familiar with the ins and outs of hiring children, along with expert guidance from financial professionals versed in the mechanics of establishing Child IRAs.

APPENDIX II. APPENDIX IV. Footnotes

Chapter 4: The Tiny Sacrifice That Will Practically Guarantee Your Child Retires a Millionaire

[1] "The State of American Dining in 2015," *Zagat's*, January 20, 2015

Chapter 10: Not Your Father's IRA – How to Open a New Child IRA for Your Child or Grandchild

[1] "*USA Weekend* calls it quits," *The Davis Enterprise*, December 28, 2014, page A3

[2] Achibee, Ashley & Beanblossom, Cheryl, "This Mother's Day, think of lifetime financial moves to help kids," *Macoupin County Enquirer-Democrat*, Thursday, May 3, 2012, page 8A

[3] https://www.fidelity.com/about-fidelity/individual-investing/fidelity-introduces-roth-ira-for-kids

[4] "Turbocharge your child's retirement with a Roth IRA for Kids," Fidelity Learning Center, https://www.fidelity.com/learning-center/personal-finance/retirement/turbocharge-childs-retirement

[5] Ibid.

Chapter 17: A Special Advantage Just For (Some) Family-Owned Businesses – Three Steps to Increase Current Family Wealth While Lowering Taxes as You Turn Your Teen Into a Millionaire

[1] https://www.statisticbrain.com/family-owned-business-statistics/ downloaded August 21, 2017

[2] http://www.fonerbooks.com/taxes/stats.htm downloaded August 21, 2017

[3] Astrachan, J.H. and Shanker, M.C. (2003), "Family Businesses' Contribution to the U.S. Economy: A Closer Look," *Family Enterprise USA*. http://www.familyenterpriseusa.com/wp-content/uploads/2016/09/FB-in-US-2003.pdf downloaded August 21, 2107

[4] "Parents Deny Kids Are Breaking Child Labor Laws By Working At Family's Pizzeria, by Emily Friedman, ABC News, May 28, 2010 http://abcnews.go.com/Business/child-labor-laws-questioned-connecticut-family-pizzeria-lawsuit/story?id=10762561 downloaded August 21, 2017

[5] "Pizza Parents Settle With State," by LeAnne Gendreau, NBC Connecticut, December 10, 2017, https://www.nbcconnecticut.com/news/local/Pizza-Parents-Settle-With-State--111461304.html downloaded August 21, 2017

[6] "Best Thin Crust New Haven Style Pizza Grand Apizza, Clinton," *Shoreline Times*, October 24, 2013

[7]http://www.ctnow.com/best-of/new-haven/local-favorites/ctn-best-of-new-haven-2015-madison-pizza-place-story.html downloaded August 21, 2017

Chapter 18: Is This the Solution to the Inevitable Social Security Crisis?

[1] "Historical Average Federal Tax Rates for All Households 1979-2013," Tax Policy Center, Urban Institute and Brookings Institution, 2016, http://www.taxpolicycenter.org/statistics/historical-average-federal-tax-rates-all-households

[2] "Fiscal Year 2014 Budget Overview," Social Security Administration, April 2013

INDEX:

ABOUT THE AUTHOR

Award-winning financial writer Christopher Carosa once exposed the soft underbelly of a trillion-dollar industry (and still has the scars to prove it). Mr. Carosa is a popular and entertaining speaker, appearing from coast to coast. Referred to by his peers as an "imbedded reporter," he has written more than a thousand feature stories, columns, and exclusive interviews as Editor-in-Chief of *FiduciaryNews.com*, a Senior Contributor for *Forbes.com*, and regular contributor to a variety of other print and digital news publications.

The author of eight books and a popular stage play, Mr. Carosa's widely acclaimed *401(k) Fiduciary Solutions* (Pandamensional Solutions, 2012) has been called "a vital reference tool for years to come." His thoughts and opinions have been sought out by such major media outlets as *The Wall Street Journal, The New York Times, USA Today, Barron's*, CNBC, CNN, and Fox Business News.

A rare breed among financial journalists, Mr. Carosa has accumulated a long, variegated, and successful record as a practitioner in the financial services industry. After earning a degree in physics and astronomy from Yale University in 1982, he joined Manning & Napier Advisers, Inc. During his 14 years there, he helped start the firm's proprietary mutual fund series, created the firm's custodial operations division, and created their trust company that accumulated nearly $1 billion in assets before he left.

Mr. Carosa earned his MBA from the Simon School at the University of Rochester and the CTFA (Certified Trust and Financial Adviser) professional designation from the Institute of Certified Bankers. Today, he is president of Carosa Stanton Asset Management, LLC, a boutique investment firm. He's also Chairman of the Board and President of Bullfinch Fund, Inc. He also serves on the Board of Directors of the New York Press Association and is Past President of the National Society of Newspaper Columnists.

If you'd like to read more by Mr. Carosa, feel free to browse his author's site, ChrisCarosa.com; LifetimeDreamGuide.com, a site to another book he's working on; his site devoted to his first love, AstronomyTop100.com; and, ChildIRA.com, where both parents and professionals can discover additional bonus material about how to explore the many advantages of The Child IRA.

Mr. Carosa lives in Mendon, NY with his wife, Betsy, three children, Cesidia, Catarina, and Peter, and their beagle, Wally.

www.ingramcontent.com/pod-product-compliance
Lightning Source LLC
Chambersburg PA
CBHW070808100426
42742CB00012B/2296